The Mathematics of the Mind

Nuri Muhammad

NURI MUHAMMAD

Printed in the United States of America.
Published by Bashirah House Publishing - First Edition, 2024
Editing / Proofreading: Traci C. Muhammad (Phoenix, AZ)
Transcription: Shareefah Muhammad (Houston, TX)
Cover/Interior/Editing: Rodney 'Asaad' Muhammad (Phoenix, AZ)

"The Mathematics of the mind means that whatever we feed the mind the most is what wins."

—Nuri Muhammad

NURI MUHAMMAD

Contents

Editor's Note

To still the mind, in a world where we must constantly endure the bombardment of discordance, is to know real power. The man or woman who fully possess their mind is a person who consistently performs at a peak level, no matter the prevailing circumstances.

In this hour, to make the conscious decision to be in a state of serenity is radical. The kind of radical that produces life altering and life lifting circumstances. To do this, we must understand that we will never be better than our thought cycle. It is a mathematical impossibility, for what we think we do indeed become. Thoughts are things—they have weight and hold space.

The mind, the ability to think your own thoughts, is a sacred and profane place. A place that should be vigilantly guarded. To place a guard, a sentinel, on our minds is to filter every thought, suggestion or idea that arises, no matter who it is from or where. *The Mathematics of the Mind*, the newest book from Bro. Nuri Muhammad, introduces the reader to three forms of sight and the two minds we each have. It is an awe-inspiring examination of the very process of thinking, from a righteous mind set. *The Mathematics of the Mind* explains how to properly calculate our outcomes based on the mathematical arc of each thought we think.

In Genesis 28:12 we read, "And he (Jacob) dreamed, and behold a ladder set up on the earth, and the top of it reached to heaven: and behold the angels of God ascending and descending on it." Through reading *The Mathematics of the Mind* we come to see that one interpretation of this profound scripture could be that the "the angels of God ascending and descending" a ladder that reaches to heaven describes the mind and the cycles of thought. Meaning, the more our mind is recalibrated around that which is truth and righteousness, we can evolve through the vicissitudes of life faster. Though we go down from the difficulties we face in life, we are always aware, that with anything of value, as the Honorable Minister Louis Farrakhan teaches us, there is a "difficulty factor."

The difficulty factor is a factor of mathematical quality and quantity that must be resolved successfully before we can proceed to the completion of the equation—which is the attainment of the goals for which we are striving. The real test of a man or a woman is how long it takes to progress from a thought to an idea, to action, to the successful manifestation of what was once just a thought. It is the resolution of this equation—thought to manifestation, that Bro. Nuri Muhammad seeks to offer tested solutions through *The Mathematics of the Mind*. Solutions that are truly attainable and actionable by anyone, no matter where we are in life. For it is true, we are always one thought away from our best and most righteous life and self.

The Saviour, Master Fard Muhammad (To Whom All Holy Praise is Due Forever) instructed the students of Muhammad University of Islam (which is all of us if we but understood),

"Let no one excel you in anything."

With the name of Allah,
The Most Gracious, the Ever Merciful
  1. Say, 'I seek refuge in the Lord of mankind,
  2. 'The Sovereign, the Controller of all affairs of mankind,
  3. 'The God of mankind,
  4. '(That He may protect me) from the evil (of the whisperings) of the whisperer, the sneaking one.
  5. 'Who whispers evil suggestions into the hearts of mankind,
  6. 'From among the jinn (-fiery natured, haughty) and the (ordinary) people.'

-- Surah 114 Al-Nas

May Allah (God), Master Fard Muhammad bless us to see the light and walk therein-*continuously*.

Your Sister,
Traci C. Muhammad
Phoenix, Arizona
February 2, 2024

NURI MUHAMMAD

Two Part Mathematics

The claim of this world's mathematicians is that mathematics can be broken down into four fundamental parts. The mathematicians claim that the four parts are "addition, multiplication, subtraction, and division." The truth is mathematics can be broken down into just two parts. How is this possible? Because the reality is, division is subtraction at a faster rate and multiplication is addition, at a faster rate. So, the fundamental parts of mathematics are subtraction and addition. The mathematics of the mind means finding the formula to subtract the negative thought material in our mind, what we do not want, and what does not serve us while we add to our mind the positive thought material that we do want. How do we subtract from the mind what we do not want? Many will claim that they know how. The real litmus test is not can we subtract from our mind the habit of smoking, the habit of overeating, the habit of lust or gambling for a few days? Can we stop all these self-destructive habits for the remainder of our lives, no matter what circumstances we face going forward.

The mathematics of the mind has all other forms of mathematics defeated. Though there are numerous people who know calculus, trigonometry, quantum physics, most of them do not know the mathematics of the mind. Architects with drug habits; Mathematicians who abuse their wives; Physicist who are liars. What this teaches us is the ability to manipulate numbers, does not necessarily mean we have the power to deal with life. The mathematical formula for the development of character, discipline, fight, drive, and focus is the highest form of mathematics of the mind, which goes untaught in the so-called institutions of higher learning. Schools of this world offer knowledge but do not recognize the all-knowing. Schools that teach how to develop machines, but not how to develop morals. Schools that teach how to build cars, but not how to build character. These are not institutions of light and light, but institutions of darkness. Institutions that produce wickedly wise people who by way of their degrees, infiltrate positions of power, manipulate the media, banking and politics and turn the whole's into a high class, technologically advanced 'Hell' on Earth.

The Honorable Minister Louis Farrakhan teaches, *"Character is the sea by which knowledge floats."* A heavy loaded ship, in shallow water, can go nowhere. Likewise, a person made heavy with knowledge but with shallow character, cannot make true progress. Whatever is obtained by doing wrong, will not last long. Not only will what the wrongdoers acquire not last, any accomplishment that they strive for absent character, morals, and principles, means the mind will functioning at a very small percentage of its true power. The Honorable Minister Louis Farrakhan writes on page100 of his illuminating book, titled **A Torchlight for America**, *"Being righteous will give us peace of mind and power. When we act in accord with what is right, we can lay down at night with the peace of mind that comes from knowing we haven't done anything or anyone wrong. This is where the true and real power of our minds comes from." The ability to focus on something, summon the power of our being to bring into reality our vision, in this time period, is truly based upon our striving to be right.* This means that the real power of the mind does not come from knowledge. Knowledge is a tool, but the power of the mind comes from righteousness. Even if the tool is the right tool for a job, if the person with the tool does not have the power to use that tool, the tool becomes ineffective. Likewise, when we have knowledge but not have morals, we are operating at a very small percentage of our mental power.

There was a Stanford study done in 1991, where they calculated the average mind power, the American people were using at that time. The statistics proved then that the American people used around 3% to 8% of their total mental power. They scientist revisited this study again in 2019 and found that the average American is now only using 2% of their mental power. There is a law, known as the Law of Use, that exists in our universe. According to the Law of Use, what you do not use, abuse, or misuse, you shall lose. So, if 98% of the mental power is going unused, abused, or misused, that mental power will be lost. All schools of mathematics are important; however, the Mathematics of the Mind is critical.

Insha'Allah (God willing), We are going to take a deep dive into this most critical subject or science and show how we can convert this potential power into kinetic energy and use it to secure a victory for ourselves, our families, and our people.

As human beings, we have two sights or ways of seeing. The first is *insight* which is the ability to perceive the present and *hindsight*, the ability to reflect on the past, properly weighing what occurred through a non-emotional perspective. A popular colloquial saying is, "hindsight is 20/20" this saying embodies the *hindsight* concept. The challenge is if the accuracy of sight is only retrospective in nature, then sight is absent the power to renegotiate the past and it does not serve us in the now. Only seeing what already has happened or occurred, and being unable to go back in time, is a perfect recipe for regret. In life, there are only two pains that man is going to suffer. Either the pain of discipline, or the pain of regret. The pain of discipline is the front-end good pain that produces reward for the *future*. Regret is a backend, negative pain that makes one feel powerless in the *present*. Therefore, our desire should be to have our *insight* be 20/20. This will cause our discipline to replace regret.

There is a third sight. It is this third sight that separates normal people from messengers of God. We as regular people have two sights insight and hindsight; however, the messengers of God are blessed with the third sight, *foresight*. The Most Honorable Elijah Muhammad and the Honorable Minister Louis Farrakhan are two divine men, servants, among us that not only have hindsight and insight, but they are also blessed by Allah (God) with a third sight: *foresight*. Meaning, not only do they have insight (present) and hindsight (past) they have foresight which means they can see the future! This concept of black people receiving a messenger has been a great psychological challenge among us as a people. This is because we have been subliminally programmed to believe it is a crime to marry black and divine or even black and good with one another! In the dictionary, when you look up the adjective black, there are 120 definitions, nearly all of them are negative. When you look up the adjective white, they are 130+ definitions, almost all of them are favorable and positive.

In Language: if you are the misfit in the family, you are the black sheep. In every movie the criminals and villains where black. At a funeral we wear black. When the Stock market crashes, they called it black Monday. Having bad luck, you're behind the 8 ball. The eight ball in pool is the black ball. Isn't it something, that in the game of pool, green felt like the Earth. There is a white ball that is larger than all the other balls on the table. The white ball is used to put all the other colored balls in their place. The eight ball is the last ball to go in on the table. If you knock it in too early, you automatically lose the game. If you are kicked out of a fraternity or sorority, they say 'you've been black balled.' Someone set you up, you were blackmailed. Angel food cake is white cake with white icing, but devil's food cake is chocolate cake with chocolate icing. Bad night – Black night. Gloomy, negative- Black Outlook. Deliberate Lie- Black Lie. No moral quality, wicked, evil- Black Hearted. If you are very, near white, you are called "Fair skinned." This is all subliminal programming.

In Religion: Every depiction of the messengers, the prophets, the angels, Jesus, whether it is a still picture or a motion picture, they tell a big white lie, and make them all white. As a Muslim, we believe in all of messengers, all of the prophets, and all of the revealed words that came from each of them. It just so happens that these pale images are not scripturally sound depictions of the messengers of God. Exodus 4:6- Moses puts his hand into the bosom of the Lord, and it is turned white. If it was turned white, his hand has to have been black before. Job 30:30 – Job says, my skin is black. Abraham in Genesis was mistaken for an Egyptian. Egypt in Greek is Aigyptos, which means land of the black and the burnt skin people. If Abraham was thought to be an Egyptian, he had to have black burnt skin. Jesus's mother, Mary was an Egyptian woman. A black woman. When they were hiding Jesus from King Herod and the authorities, Jesus fled into Egypt to hide. Another word for hide is camouflage. When you are camouflaging, you are blending in with the predominate color of the environment. When the army is in the snow, they wear white because it blends in with the color of the environment. When they are in the desert, they wear beige. In the jungle, green. When they are on a mission, they wear black because it blends in with the predominate color of the environment.

Jesus was in the land of the black and burnt skin people and did not get caught or captured. He was there to hide, to use the natural landscape—in this case people, to successfully camouflage himself, and evade capture. To evade capture in Egypt by camouflage, then Jesus had to be black too. We read in Revelation that Jesus had hair like lamb's wool and feet like brass burned in an oven. Paul said, in Romans 1:3 Jesus was the seed of David according to the flesh. Jesus said in Revelations 22:16 "I am of the root and offspring of David." David had a son named Solomon. *Son* is from the seed of or the offspring of. Solomon 1:6 – Solomon says, "I am Black." If Solomon was of the seed and offspring of David, like Jesus said of himself, and he was black, then Jesus would have to be black also. This erroneous ideological stance of Jesus being white is one of the most destructive lies ever told to the black psyche.

Divine Distribution

Let us take a closer look at this through the lens of the mathematics of the mind. Mathematically, if Jesus is white and he is the son of God, then God is his father, which means He would have to be white too. God is good and God is love and God is white, and we are the opposite of white, then we are the opposite of God. None of us has said this out loud, but the mental mathematics of the subconscious mind still has worked this equation. Black pain and white pain is not the same kind of pain. We suffer from a depression that comes from oppression and suppression. White supremacy oppresses combined with a suppression of the truth about the origin of blackness, the blackness that is self. <u>Buddha</u> was a black man. Zaha of Japan was a black man. Fu His of China was a black man. TYR of Scandinavia was a black man; Quetzalcóatl of Mexico was black man. The Honorable Minister Louis Farrakhan teaches us, that the pattern of God is consistent, and the Bible bears him witness. Malachi 3:6 says, "I am the Lord I do not change." The divine distribution system of the creator, the primary instrument for God's inspiration and instruction has always been the black man and black woman. God has been speaking through a black man for trillions of years. It is time for us to stop playing and recognize that God did it again. The divine distributor of the word, will, and way of God is a black man among us named the Honorable Minister Louis Farrakhan!

This is why we do not need to expend significant amounts of energy trying to figure out how to do this thing we call life. Why? Because Allah (God) has already revealed how to live, and His formula covers every dimension and aspect of time. Which means no matter what prevailing circumstances seem to rule the time, Allah's (God's) formula covers them all, *without exception*. The Allah's (God's)formula encompasses **four divine principles** which never change or alter. The scholars call this, the 'Universal Message' of the

Messengers. These principles are to *do good, do right, avoid evil* and *treat people good.* Inside each of these principles are specific habits, that each messenger Allah (God) has raised over time, is given to help the people deal with the level of wickedness, evil and devilishment they must confront. Every messenger of God is given a contemporary message with the universal message. The contemporary message provides real time revelation that has factored in the magnitude of Satan in the time period that the messenger is teaching. There is a saying that says, "yesterday' s keys cannot open up today's lock," and "the higher at the level, the bigger the devil."

According to the Scripture in the book of Genesis, Satan begins as a *serpent* but the next time we find Satan is in the 22nd book of the Bible—the book of Isaiah Satan has grown and evolved into a Leviathan. From this stage of development, Satan becomes known as a *beast.* By the time the enemy of God, Satan, matures, in the book of Revelations, the last book, he is called a *dragon* and has *a tail.* Scripture indicates that his tail, not his entire body, but his tail, is so powerful that his tail can knock out a third of the stars.

Reality check, this not Looney Toons, Nick Jr., some anime cartoon, or imaginative fictionalized non-reality we are dealing with. There is no big ole' dragon in the sky with a tail so big and powerful, it can knock out the little lights we see at night, called stars. The Honorable Elijah Muhammad teaches us that the stars mentioned here in scripture represent the wisest scientists of God. This means that Satan has matured (developed) to a level that his tail, just the end part of his weaponry, is so powerful that he can *trick* the wisest scientists of God.

Surely, if we are living in the time of revelation, fighting a dragon, we do not want to come to the battlefield as though we are fighting the serpent that was originally in the garden. Taking nothing to the battlefield but a stick, thinking we straight, only to show up and find a dragon. When we were coming up, we used to say, 'don't get caught bringing a knife to a gun battle.' Though we did not mean it literally, what we really meant was, in warfare, no matter what level, we have to assess the magnitude and overall capacity of our opponent and show up accordingly, otherwise, we would be taking a guaranteed 'L'.

Allow me to illustrate this point further; have you ever seen a fighter who underestimated his opponent? In the pre-fight interviews the reporter asks, *"You mean to tell me you're gonna accept this fight on a two-week notice?"* Wait, what do you mean? Why is this a question? Because, you have not been training. You have not been studying your opponent deeply enough to learn their weaknesses and strengths. You have not developed reflex guards for the opponents strengths nor figured out how to exploit his weaknesses. The fighter who takes a fight with a 10-day, 2-week notice says, "Oh, he ain't nothing. He ain't got nothing but one punch. He got a good left hook. That ain't nothing! Fought plenty of people with a good left hook and they down."

The fighter shows up without training; unprepared. Underestimating the opponent and next thing you know, knockout! And when the fight is over, hindsight is always 20/20, *"I shouldn't have accepted it. I should've trained. He got more than a left hook. He got a right cross and a mean uppercut. I didn't know his footwork was like that. I didn't know he had that kind of speed on him."* This is the perfect illustration of I came to the fight ready to deal with a serpent in a garden, but I should have been training because the fight was actually against a dragon. So, it is when a Messenger of God is raised among the people. God does an assessment of His own enemy and calculates the moves of His own enemy and then gives the community that accepts and believes in Him, through His Messenger, the formula for how they can get the best out of life and win against the devil. All Praise is due to Allah.

I know it is hard to believe that God cared enough about Black people to raise *us* up a Messenger. The real question is what makes you think we would not get a Messenger, Black people in America? Hell, if the God we believe in is the kind of God that is only willing to work 4,000 years ago, in the past, with a Moses, or 2,000 years ago with Jesus, or 1,400 years ago with Prophet Muhammad (PBUH) 9,000 miles away in Saudi Arabia, this is not a God I want to believe in. How can we identify a people engaged in idol worship and give them an Abraham 5,000 years ago. A people fighting and killing one another and give them Noah 5,500 years ago. A people in bondage and give them Moses 4,000 years ago. People that have lost respect for their women and have an alcohol problem and give them Prophet Muhammad (PBUH) 1400 years ago.

Here we are, the black man and woman in America, idol worshipping. Sodom and Gomorrah look like a friendly neighborhood with the amount of freakishness that goes on around America. Ancient Egypt has nothing on America. Ancient Rome has nothing on Washington D.C. We are suffering from all the conditions that brought birth to each Messenger in the past. Malachi 3:6 teaches us that God is the "Lord and changeth not" so we must ask where is our Messenger?

Ours is present. His name is The Most Honorable Elijah Muhammad, and his second self is The Honorable Minister Louis Farrakhan. The new cut man. The new trainer. The new manager. The one that is going to give us the encouraging words we need; the discipline we need; the formula we need. Not to deal with a serpent but to deal with a full-grown dragon. A dragon that possesses chemtrails, biological weaponry, who has manipulated the air, the food and the water. A dragon that has convinced people to think thoughts that did not come from their own mind, that they never heard, never read themselves as though they are their own. A dragon that knows how to manipulate people by manipulating the very atmosphere.

And while we know this to be the current prevailing reality, we do not need to worry or stress. Why, because if we are following **How to Eat to Live,** we have the formula. What formula? The formula to overcome the manipulation of the atmosphere and the very food we eat. The formula is as follows: fast three days a month, eat one meal per day. Stay away from evil. Eat navy bean soup, whole wheat bread, drink a glass of pure milk and eat vegetables. Treat people right and watch Allah (God) bless us to come to this battle with the dragon and win.

THE MATHEMATICS OF THE MIND

Two Different Brains

The Most Honorable Elijah Muhammad is blessed with foresight and as result he taught us and said so much the enemy is only recently catching up to these divine truths. In 1929, in numerous scientific journals, if you looked up the word atom, it was defined as the smallest particle of matter. However, go forward just two (2) years to 1931 and the definition changed. An atom no longer equaled the smallest particle of matter. By 1931 the new prevailing belief was that an atom could be cracked to reveal other subatomic particles. Subatomic particles which contain the very same protons, neutrons and electrons which allow it to operate with the same level of power, like a whole atom, though it is much smaller.

The Most Honorable Elijah Muhammad was *told* in 1930, that a single atom could be successfully cracked into10 million parts. At the time, the prevailing thought was that the smallest particle of matter was the atom; however, the scientist kept refining the number which they were able to do because they finally cracked an atom. What the scientist of this world found on the inside of the cracked atom, was the quark, which still contained the power of an atom, though it was smaller. Then they cracked the quark, and discovered the subatomic particle now called the 'quantum.' Quantum is a scientific word which means *thought*. The Honorable Elijah Muhammad teaches that around 78 trillion years ago, nothing existed in the Universe but the *thought* of God - *material darkness and electricity.*

If the quantum is the smallest particle they agree is in existence and quantum is a scientific word for thought, what the scientists of this world are agreeing to is that everything came and comes from thought. The mathematics of moving numbers is not the highest form of mathematics. The mathematics of moving the mind is the highest form of mathematics.

While there is much more, we can highlight from the Most Honorable Elijah Muhammad's Divine Teachings that the world of science is just catching up to for now let us focus on a particular area. That which is attached to the power of the human mind, that The Most Honorable Elijah Muhammad was given by God, that this world has yet to come into the knowledge, let alone the understanding of.

The Most Honorable Elijah Muhammad teaches that the brain of man is infinite. Surely, he was not speaking of the physical muscle found inside the skull, because if you go to the hospital and the doctors say there is swelling in the brain this indicates a serious problem. The Most Honorable Elijah Muhammad teaches that there is a calculable difference in the weight of the grafted man's brain and the weight of the Original man's brain. He teaches that the grafted man or Caucasian has 6 ounces (6 oz) of grafted brain. And the Original man has 7 and ½ ounces (7 ½ oz) of original brain; *two different brains*.

Six ounces of grafted brain. While we have 7 and ½ ounces of Original brain. Two different brains. Yet, for thousands of years, the physical brain of man has averaged 3 pounds (3 lbs). So, the physical brain does not weight 6 or 7 ½ ounces. When the Most Honorable Elijah Muhammad classified the weight of the brain differentiating one as grafted and one as Original, what he is explaining does not refer to the physical brain what he has given us is the different weights of the *mind*. Understand, the brain of man is infinite. The mind of man is infinite.

Everything else in the Universe is finite, limited, and temporary. The only thing that exists in the Universe, that is infinite is God, Himself. This means we can identify two things in the Universe, which exist, that are qualified to wear the title of infinite. *One is God and the other brain or mind.*

Let me ask a question. If you are infinite, then would you want a home that matches your own nature? So, where would God live? If Allah (God) is infinite and the only other thing in the Universe that is infinite is the human mind, then Allah's (God's) house is not on cloud nine somewhere around the corner from the planet ZibZab. Allah's (God's) house is inside the head of you and I. Several scriptures bear witness and prove this fact, for example Jesus said the kingdom of God is within (Luke 17:20-21) and the kingdom of heaven is within according to Matthew 13:44-46. The kingdom of God and the kingdom of heaven is within, and heaven means the highest part of where God lives (dwells).

In the Holy Qur'an we read in Surah (chapter) 11, *"Surely the throne of Allah's power is established on water. That He might manifest the great qualities within you."* This does not mean that there is a big gold chair with the Lord sitting on it in the middle of the ocean. What it does mean is that the brain sits (floats) on water. If it was God living in the ocean, then He would be posted up out there right now. Sitting on a throne, on the water manifesting the great qualities in the Atlantic Ocean. If God intends to manifest the great qualities in you and I, this means God lives in our brain. Does science not refer the two sides of human head as the 'temples?' The Temples. The temple is where God lives.

The Lord of the Worlds, teaches the Honorable Minister Louis Farrakhan, chooses a home that matches the nature of Himself. If one is clean, neat, and organized and we look for a place to live and someone says, *"Here you go. Here's a place for rent."* You go do the walk through and find the place dirty, disorganized, and damaged, what would you say? *"No thank you. That's okay."* Why? Because we want to live in a home that matches our nature or what we like. This is critical: if we know the kingdom of God is within then what kind of house are we inviting Him into? Does it match the nature of what He is? He is Honorable, He is honest, He is clean. He is productive, He is powerful, all these things. Well, when He comes to look at us, to examine us, will He have to say, *"No thank you. That's okay?"*

When we look at the term *'kingdom'*, The Honorable Minister Louis Farrakhan teaches that kingdom, *"It really is a compound word. It is 'king' and then 'dom'."* As the dome is the round part that exists at the top of a structure, so is the human head. The king-dom of God is within you and if God is the King in our dome, we live in heaven. But if the devil is the king in our dome, we live in hell.

When we really understand and know this, we no longer ask anyone whether God runs things or whether Satan runs things. We need only examine what kind of life are we living? Do we have peace and contentment of mind? Do we have harmony and balance with others? Do we have luxury, money, good homes? Do we have friendship in all walks of life? *"No, well sometimes. Well, a little bit."* If we have a little bit of this and a little bit of the other, this means the majority of the time the devil is ruling, and sometimes God is ruling. When the God becomes the king in our dome, we will not only live in heaven, but we will leave a little heaven behind everywhere we go!

What We Feed The Mind

The Mathematics of the mind means that whatever we feed the mind the most is what wins. If a thought becomes a word, and a word becomes an action, actions become habits, habits make character, character makes future then we have to be consciously downloading information that creates peace and harmony. *"Finally, brethren, whatsoever things are true, whatsoever things are honest, whatsoever things are just, whatsoever things are pure, whatsoever things are lovely, whatsoever things are of good report; if there be any virtue, and if there be any praise, think on these things"* Philippians 4:8 Our minds are made up of the deposits that we put in. These types of thoughts are called *tonic thoughts*. False hood, lies, unjust, impure, hateful, gossip and slander or all *toxic thoughts*. That which is tonic heals, and that which is toxic kills. In chapters to come, we will go deeper into these two types of thoughts and foods, "Tonic and Toxic." The words, actions, habits, and character that would come from thinking these types of tonic thoughts will allow our hands to absolutely sit us in heaven at once and the toxic thoughts will set us in hell just as fast.

Special Note: When these self-destructive, spirit killing, toxic thoughts began to show up in our mind, we have the authority over our mind to tell our mind, "go get me a better thought!" In 2 Corinthians 10:5, we read, to bring every thought 'captive unto Christ.' This means we have the authority, ability, and the assignment to arrest every thought and compare it to the mind of God. If it matches, keep it. If it does not match the mind of God, kill it! This is a practical application process to *"letting this mind be in you, the same man that was in Christ Jesus"* and *"being not conformed to the way of this world but being transformed by the renewing of the mind." "Leaning not on thine own understanding but in all thy ways acknowledging Him."* And as stated in the Holy Quran 2:138, *"We take Allah's colour, and who is better than Allah at colouring, and we are His worshippers."* When you break down the etymological route of colour, it is different than the word color. Colour means the spiritual and mental perception, not physical colors. This regiment of mental martial arts will grant us a black belt in Mind Control!

On page 105 of the monumental and illuminating book, **The Innerviews of The Honorable Minister Louis Farrakhan: Closing the Gap,** not interview. Because when you conduct an interview, you are asking about, however, if you are doing an innerview, you are asking what makes them what they are. On page 105 the Honorable Minister Louis Farrakhan's teaches about the brain, *"The cells of the brain, as the Honorable Elijah Muhammad taught us, were and are created by God to think rightly. One cannot think rightly except that the basis of a thought is on the actual or that which is factual. So, the student must always search for the real, the truth, the actual facts."*

Recently, we were walking through a particular neighborhood, and we actually could not see the faces of the people, but based on the sound we could hear, we knew there were Black people in the garage area of the home. I said, "That's Black people talking." one of the other FOI asked me, "How can you tell," because they did not sound Black, meaning they were not speaking what is known as ebonics. These were African Americans. Some of us recognize there is a difference between an African American and Black person. These were African Americans. (smile)

Again, the question came, *"How can you tell?"* I said, *"Because we are the only people who invest this much energy into gossip. Listen to how much force they are speaking suspicion. You can hear how much excitement they have and how committed they are to something that they don't even know if it's true or not."* As we got closer, we waved, and it was us. Now you know if thinking about gossip or hearing it from somebody else messes up the brain, then we must realize that speaking it, not only is it going to mess up the brain and ears of the one that heard it, but this also messes up the brain of the one who spoke it even more.

The Honorable Minister Louis Farrakhan teaches that the brain cells were created to think rightly. Right, according to the dictionary is defined as morally correct or factual. Right also can be defined as the direction of motion. The brain cells were created to think right can be viewed from two sides. One, brain cells were created to think morally correct, truthful, and factual. However, on the other side, the thought that is moving, so teaches The Honorable Elijah Muhammad, at an average speed of 24 billion miles per second around 14 billion brain cells, if all the brain cells are circular and begin to move or flow right then they are moving clockwise. Therefore, if in the brain of man, the cells were created to think moral, correct, true, factual and move at 24 billion miles per second, in clockwise direction, what happens when lies are inserted into the brain of someone whose cells were made to think right? The motion of thought is going in the opposite direction.

When we drive a car we drive in the drive gear, if we keep slamming the car in reverse, then it is only a matter of time before the car's transmission is damaged. Once the transmission is damaged what has actually occurred is the interpretation box, which allows your car to change speed and go in different directions, has been damaged. So, it is with the human brain. After a certain amount of lies have been told to the brain, we damage the transmission signals of the body's ability to go where we want it to go at the speed, we want it to go. When we see everybody else going places at a certain speed and we cannot make it, it becomes very discouraging. What do we say, *"Hell, I'm going somewhere else."*

When the brain has been fed a heavy diet of lies. It now has damaged the transmission. Perhaps, you have never had a car where the mechanic told you the transmission was slipping before. However, when a transmission starts slipping, though there maybe five gears with each gear representing fifteen miles of maximum speed. For those who do not know, when you hear that 'hmmmmm,' then you hear that or that 'emmmmm' type of sound, this is what it sounds like when switching to the next gear.

It you are in a car and your car goes 'hmmmmm' 'emmmmm' and then the next gear goes 'hmmmmmmmmmmmmmmm' and stays there and you are not gaining more speed, your transmission is messed up. Meaning, no matter how hard you hit the gas, no matter how good the rpm's rev up, you cannot go faster than what you are doing because the gears will not shift. When the human brain is fed lies, gossip, slander, and negative things, it begins to damage the ability of the brain to think what we want to think and say it correctly, think what we want to think and get it done. How long does it take for us to get things done? How long does it take for us to be able to figure things out? All of this is directly connected to transmission.

The Honorable Minister Louis Farrakhan goes on to say, *"The Honorable Elijah Muhammad told me once that it takes 500 seconds or 8 minutes and 20 seconds for the light traveling at 186,000 miles per second to travel from the Sun to the Earth. Likewise,* " He said, *"it takes 500 seconds, 8 minutes and 20 seconds, for the blood to make a complete circulation between the heel and the brain and back."* This is absolutely powerful! Scientists have discovered each person has about 60,000 miles of arteries in the body. So, The God, Master Creator, knows how to take blood through all these veins and arteries, send it all the way to the bottom, back up to the top and back to the bottom in 8 minutes and 20 seconds.

The Honorable Minister Louis Farrakhan goes on to state, *"When you go to visit a person that is sick,"* all of our antenna should go up with that statement because the truth is they are actually putting illness in the water. Have you noticed that everybody seems to be sick all the time now? Everybody all of a sudden has eczema. Everybody has asthma. Everybody literally has something going on, something wrong. Now when we get a cold, the cold lasts for two weeks. Get the flu and it lasts for a year. *"When you go to visit a person that is sick if you put the right word in their ear, within 8 minutes and 20 seconds, you will see a change in the spirit of such persons. What this told me,"* he says, *"is that the level of energy, light and spiritual power that is contained in the right words communicated from the right motivation, energizes the brain of the recipient of such word. That energy is delivered to every part of the body and thereby increasing the energy level of that person."*

Anytime we have a major impediment, the doctors of this world want to put us on a steroid. What does a steroid do? A steroid speeds up the time of your healing; however, the side effects are that though it speeds up the time of your life. What this means, mathematically, is that if it initially took the human body, without the steroid, 3 months to heal once the steroid is taken, then somebody stole 3 months of life from you just to get you right. There is a spiritual steroid, with no side effects. It is the right word coming from the right heart with the right motive. Understand, when you really love someone and you want to see them better and you know the right things to say to them, you can do more for them in the healing process, when you speak the right words, than any doctor or hospital can do for them.

The Honorable Minister Louis Farrakhan goes on to say, *"As I looked at what The Honorable Elijah Muhammad was saying to me, I recognized that there were levels of conversation that carried varying degrees of electrical energy. The lowest form of conversation which takes away from the energy of the human being and causes that persons' shoulders to droop, their face to drop, their countenance to change, the body to react, is conversation that is negative dealing with slander, backbiting and gossip. This type of conversation, which is so disruptive to unity, to brotherhood, to social relationships that affects the highest level of civilization."*

We must do a better job of encouraging each other. Allow me to point out something here, there is so much wrong with all of us, if you want to get your magnifying glasses or binoculars out, the only thing you will 'discover' is that every human being has flaws, faults, and defects. If you want to highlight all the negative things about people and tell them what they could have been and should have been and need to do, you can do that forever! Remember this wife, remember this husband, it is more important to praise what you want to raise than it is to criticize and critique what you do not want more of. We should never spend so much time talking about what a person needs to do, and what I wish you would do, or you need to be better at and when you gon do XYZ. A better more effective strategy is every time the person does what you like, praise them for it and you will find that people naturally lean toward wherever action or activity gained the applause.

If the person does something you like, even if it is once a year, praise it if you want to raise it. Praise it enough, the one or two times that they do it, and you will find in the next month it will go from two times a year to two times a month. Then when it comes up twice a month, you praise it again, make over it again, encourage again. Next thing you know the next month it goes to six times a month. At a certain point everything you want, that you have praised, you have raised it in value, and it now occupies all the space and time. Now, because you have used this strategy, they do not do any of the behaviors you disliked. Mathematics of the mind. I know some will say, Brother Nuri, you do not know my wife, may husband said, *"If I do all that, he/she still gon be stuck on stupid."* Well, another formula needs to be worked.

The Honorable Minister Louis Farrakhan goes on to explain, ***"When Almighty God, Allah, reveals a word, or what is called divine revelation that unearths secrets of Himself and His creation, that man and the wisest of men have not discovered up until that time, no matter how high the wise have gone with their wisdom and their ability to communicate their wisdom, when God so chooses to raise an individual and give that individual divine revelation, that is akin to putting the highest wattage of electricity in the head of that human being. The human being that comes at the end of the world does not only have a high wattage, but he is compared to the light of the Sun, which carries life, light, energy and warmth to all of creation. Therefore, no creature can live without the energy of the Sun. Nothing of life would survive without such energy. This one that comes at the end of the world that says that he is the Light of the world, his brain is filled with the highest form of energy. Then transmission of that light to those who walk in darkness or to those who function on a low level has the power to raise their level of conversation, their level of thought and their level of activity."*** Do you see the <u>fusion</u> going on?

Allah (God) has given the highest form of electrical energy in the revelation that we know as the Divine Teachings of The Most Honorable Elijah Muhammad. These Teachings are perfected and at the highest rate in the brain of The Master, The Messenger, and The Minister. However, The Master, The Messenger and The Minister have been opening their mouth, allowing the energy to be transmitted in lectures. Transmitted in book form and all we must do is listen to it, read it and we are able to deposit the same energy God put in them into us.

Conversations and Thoughts

As we look deeper into three specific areas, we want to start with *conversation*. When we examine corporate America, we find that in relationships, the number one cause of problems is communication. The Honorable Minister Louis Farrakhan teaches that 90% of the problems in relationships are rooted in communication, 90%! How many terms have we had to say, '*Naw, I didn't mean it like that. That's not what I was trying to say. You're taking it all wrong. Now, I know that's how it came out but what I was saying was....No, no, now wait a minute. What I was trying to say, I might have called you that, but I don't really think you're that. You know I don't see...I don't think you that. No, no, if I did, I wouldn't, I wouldn't even buy you clothes and...*' And what's the response: *Well, buying clothes and putting a roof over the head of people whatever cuz you can do that for dogs and fish. That don't mean..."*

In our **Supreme Wisdom Lessons**, Master Fard Muhammad writes, ***"You will not be successful unless you do speak well."*** Not good. <u>Well</u>. Speaking good is subject verb agreement—the actual articulation of the words. *Speaking well is saying the right thing at the right time to get the best result.* Which means the formula is: We will <u>not</u> be successful unless we do speak <u>well</u>, if we do speak well, we <u>will</u> be successful.

Next, we must raise our level of ***thought***. It is a fact that across the board, all persons of wealth and power always want to live or work from the highest floor in all the buildings. Even Jeff Bezos and the Elan Musk, the super-rich. Sir Richard Branson owns Virgin Records and several other companies, but what does he want to do? Mr. Branson, Mr. Bezos and Mr. Musk all have the same desire, born form the fact that they have been in penthouses and the highest floors in buildings around the world, now their next obsession: *"I want to go into outer space. I want to be as high up as I can be."*

Have you noticed, that when you go to check into a hotel and say, "I want the best room you have." It's never next to the candy store. Or two doors down from the gift shop. The presidential suite is on the highest floor. Why? Because it gives one the view of everything. The optics change so that which looks large when you are near it looks small the higher up you are. This applies not just to the super rich, go downtown to whatever building serves as the city hall and ask where the mayor's office is. The mayor's office is on the highest floor in the building. They want to be up. Why? Because the higher up you are, optics, the visual changes. Then if the mind or the thought pattern can be raised by tuning into revelation, which means what others consider to be a big struggle, a big problem, something hard to do or hard to achieve, becomes small to you. And as a direct consequence, the level of activity correspondingly as well.

Returning to the, the Honorable Minister Louis Farrakhan words, he states, ***"When such a person is communicating to somebody that is dead, then the person who is considered dead is functioning on the lowest level of human behavior and human conversation or communication. They have not received that which would raise them in thought and in action from where they are. When a man like that appears, a messenger of God, The Messiah, then to feed on his word that comes directly from God is to feed our brain the best food; the highest form of food."***

To purchase a performance automobile, the reality is that it is counterproductive to put a cheap source of energy (cheap gas) in a high-performance engine. The human brain is a high, exceedingly high creation that functions best when it is fed from the highest energy source. Man's connection to God is life itself and his disconnect from that source of the highest energy, is death. When we are blessed with a man who has received divine revelation and we breathe in or inhale such wisdom, the brain cells began to operate at the highest level of efficiency. The word efficiency is defined as speed meaning smooth—without a challenge. Moving at an exceedingly high rate of speed yet it is a smooth ride.

If we fail to become a god and a nation of gods, it will not be because we were not well taught. The Honorable Minister Louis Farrakhan is the greatest teacher that the world has ever seen. Never has there been another human being that can articulate the truth in a way that excites in the hearer the believability that you can be what you are hearing and learning like the Honorable Minister Louis Farrakhan does.

Our thoughts expressed in conversation has an effect on our mind and in our bodies. When we change the energy of our self-expression—our internal dialogue, then though toxins may be in our body and mind, though poisons may be there, though dull thought may be there, once there is a connection to the highest form of energy contained in divine revelation, the brain begins to oscillate, to vibrate, to function at its highest level. The Law of Physics teaches us that two things cannot occupy the same space at the same time. The more it (our mind) feeds from that source (divine revelation) the stronger the brain becomes, the greater its sight, the greater its hearing, the greater its ability to think and plan and bring into existence what it plans. Satan then recognizes that this is the end of his world, when the dead receive the life-giving word contained in divine revelation.

Satan then must enter the equation." Mathematics of the mind. Satan enters the equation to cause the person not to think on or dwell on, conversate about the divine revelation. Satan's job is to turn the mind away from the high thing and turn it towards sex, turn it toward material acquisition, *turn it toward low things. Then Satan has a chance to take the mind where he wants to take it in contravention to where God wants to take the human being.* Mathematics of the mind.

Thoughts: Electrochemical Energy

We have heard a lot about a developing technology referred to as artificial intelligence. Artificial Intelligence is defined as a replica of the original intelligence or the human mind. The computer is a copy of the brain and the rule of occupational expectancy of any device is called gigo. GIGO is an acronym, which stands for *garbage in, garbage out*. How do you know garbage in, garbage out? Remember our life in our mind turned inside out. Remember, you cannot get out of a thing what is not already in it—in its very nature. The dictionary defines the word, garbage as contemptibly worthless, vile, with one of the definitions being **inferior**. In the previous chapter, we examined the source of the highest level of energy, finding that it comes from conversation. So, Supreme Wisdom produces Supreme actions, and Supreme actions, produce a Supreme life. Inferior, which is under the category of garbage, will produce inferior actions and then an inferior life. Whatever we want on the outside, we must put on the inside. Did you know that a computer uses electricity and so does the brain? Electrical waves travel through the computer and electricity travels at a high speed through the nervous system of the brain and the body.

A computer operates using electricity, yet it can catch a virus. For a computer to catch a virus, generally, searches were being conducted on sites that left the computer vulnerable to attack. When a computer catches a virus, the screen freezes. It slows down. It stops working properly. The brain operates using electricity also. The question is, what can give the brain a virus? Downloading information or images that are not in alignment with the true nature of the brain cell, which is created to think right, morally correct, true, good and factual. Did you know that you cannot make a statement and when asked *'how do you know it's true'*, you cannot say, *"Because I got it off the internet."* There is no moral police force checking facts on the internet. It is not the knowledge superhighway; it is the information superhighway. Information could be wrong.

What makes the brain different from a computer is that the brain also uses chemicals to transmit information, and this is where the food we eat comes in. The digestive system is designed to take solids and turn them into liquids. The goal of digestion is to take what we consume, break it down to its chemical form and then distribute those chemicals (nutrients) all over the body and give the body what it needs to function at an optimal state. This means the food we eat, once it transforms to the chemical state travels through the blood: every 8 minutes and 20 seconds, it can make one complete circulation throughout the body. From the sole of the foot to the crown of the head, through the brain, and back down.

What happens when we are eating bad food? Thoughts are electrochemical energy, fast moving fluids. When we eat bad food, and it breaks down to the chemical state, the chemicals of the food mix with the nature of our thoughts. We can then catch a virus from bad websites, but we can also catch a virus from a bad lunch or a bad dinner.

A computer's memory grows by adding computer chips. The memory of the brain grows stronger by synaptic connections. What makes synaptic connections? There are three things the brain needs for it to grow. Fuel, oxygen, and stimulation. The fuel is knowledge. The fuel is good food. Oxygen is clean air. Let me know when you find some clean air. And stimulation, stimulation from the brain comes in four basic ways; mental exercise, we generally knew that because a cornerstone of all levels of education is playing memory games, memorizing things, testing ourselves to see what we remember by study and quizzes. That activity is mental exercise. Reading is also a mental exercise.

What many do not know is that physical exercise strengthens the brain. The science of this can be read more deeply in a book entitled *Spark*. In that book the reader is introduced to multiple studies where people who suffer from clinical depression, anxiety, stress, and numerous other forms of mental and physical ailments were prescribed, not a drug but an exercise regimen. By following the exercise regimen, they were able to defeat these impediments by exercise alone.

The stimulation of the brain comes from work. Work is not just the motion of doing something. Work is force X distance. Which means we are doing something (activity), but we have a goal to get from where we are to where we want it to be. The mental satisfaction that comes from moving an object from where it is to where you want it to be feeds the brain.

Many people love being victims and playing the role of victim. One of the worst states to find ourselves in is when we enjoy the comfort we receive from people when we are suffering, more than we enjoy the mental satisfaction that comes from accomplishing things we want to do. The minute we get more mental satisfaction out of people hugging us and crying with us, consoling us all the time, next thing we know our brain begins to say we feel good. This feeling is addictive and the only time we then feel good is when someone comes and consoles us, but we only get this comfort, this type of ease, when something is wrong, so subconsciously we create situations where we have something wrong to place us in a position to receive the comfort that comes with this. Even if nothing is wrong, we will make something wrong. *A victim gets mental satisfaction from the sympathy of others. A victor gets mental satisfaction from achievement.*

Every day we wake up, we are faced with one or two choices, make moves, or make excuses. When we go through trials, sometimes we like to deceive ourselves into thinking that my trial is so unique that no one would ever understand what I am going through nor has anyone ever gone through what I am going through. This particular verse has always recalibrated my thinking and kept me from crossing over into the victim role/mode. 1 Corinthians 10:13 (NLT), *"The temptations in your life I no different from what other experience. And God is faithful. He will not allow the temptation to be more than you can stand. When you are tempted, He will show you a way out so that you can endure."* **Dear brothers and sisters, no matter what has happened or what has been done to us by others, we have one choice, we can either become wise, or we can become wounded!** When we become wise from it, we operate with more power in the present. When we become wounded, we become handicap by what has happened, operating with less power in the present to make what we want happen.

What feeds the brain is physical exercise, mental exercise, and social interaction. Social interaction what does this mean? Social Interaction refers to how well we get along with people. According to the scriptures, when God completed creating the universe--sun, moon, stars, planet creatures, etc. He called all of these things, "a" glory of God. When He created men, He called us "The" glory of God. "The" is the definite article that means the supreme, the top, the greatest, the best, the most. So, the supreme creation that should be handled with the most care and sought after to be in communion with, should not found in the things of this world, but the beings of this world, our brothers and sisters. The Caucasian, Eurocentric, non-spiritual world of materialism, has us loving things and using people, when we should be loving people, and using things! Allah (God) teaches in the Holy Qur'an that the human being was created to be a social being. In the Holy Qur'an we learn that Allah (God) created everything in communities. We are born to be people persons. Only a person that is out of balance with self says *'I'm not a people person. I don't really like people.'* No, understand what is really being said, the person is really saying I do not like being let down or disappointed or being tricked and deceived. The pain associated with unfulfilled expectations is so great that now I do not think I can bear it. The reality is we should never allow the idea of the reciprocity we get in life to come from the horizontal. Look for reciprocity to come from the vertical.

When we do good by and for other people, the Holy Quran says, *do no good seeking gain.* This means we should not keep score. Do not spend time trying to measure if they have done their part back to you in like measure. Know that Allah (God) judges and He is the best of judges. No good deed goes without its just reward. So, even if no one ever gives you your reciprocity, **the governor of reciprocity is not your son, or daughter, husband, or wife. The governor of reciprocity is The Lord of Worlds** and He will never shortchange you or me. Social interaction, we must be kind and good to others.

Jesus teaches, *"I came not into the world to be served but I came to serve. Let him who is going to be chief among you be your servant."* What does this really mean? The best person is the one that is out trying to do for other people, they are putting service above self. Never worry about getting back everything that you do. Do it for The Lord of the Worlds. Do it because you are blessed to be a blessing. You got it, share it and Allah's (God) will bless you. However, if we keep on training our mind in the direction that says that your blessings will come from the person you loaned the money to, the son you raised, or the daughter you raised you will be disappointed always. All good deeds are accounted for by Allah (God). The Believer says, *"The only place I am looking for recognition and blessings is from Allah (God), and I will wait for Him to provide because Allah is the best of providers."*

Friends? How Many of Us Have Them?

An additional aspect of social interaction is choosing the right kinds of people as friends. A question was raised via X (formerly known as Twitter) *What is the definition of a true friend?"* This is something we all need to know. Because everybody had a friend, at some point, and we no longer have them as a friend. What happened? Very few people have friends that they have had their entire life.

The Honorable Minister Louis Farrakhan defines a true friend, ***"One cannot be a friend of man until and unless we become a friend of God, and you cannot become a friend of God until we love Him with all our hearts, soul, mind and strength. Then the scripture teaches you become a servant of others."*** The math here teaches us that our friendships must be based upon the morals and the righteousness of a person. We cannot be around people who are the opposite of what we are trying to be and become.

Never should we lay down the banner of Savior. Do not get to a point where you do not want to redeem people, where you do not want to be around people that are not on your level. *"Got to be on the same energy that I'm on."* No, find people that do not have energy and give them the energy that the man gave you when you did not have any. A mirror reflects a man's face, but who a person really is, is shown by the kind of friends that they choose.

Proverbs 27:19, 1st Corinthians 13:33 says, *"Do not be deceived, bad company ruins good morals."* Surah 24:26 says, ***"Unclean things are for unclean ones and unclean ones are for unclean things. Good things are for good ones and good ones are for good things. These are free from what they say, for them is*** *forgiveness and an honorable sustenance.*" We cannot tell others we are something different if everybody we are close with are what they are.

Solomon said, *"If you walk with the wise, you become wise, for a companion of fools will suffer harm."* **"Let not the believers take the disbelievers for friends, rather than believers and whoever does this has no connection with Allah."** None! Surah 3:28. Muhammad was asked which friends are best. He said, **"Whosever sight reminds you of Allah, whose conversation adds to your knowledge and whose actions help you remember the hereafter."** Stimulation, social interaction.

To fix a computer you must get new parts. We fix our life by getting a new mind. The beauty of the human brain lies in something called neuroplasticity. Neuroplasticity means the capacity of the nervous system to develop new neuro connections which is a self-correction mechanism. All it takes is for us to just make up our mind that I am going to start thinking right, speaking right, eating right and doing right. Automatically, our body goes into healing mode. We can be healed from anything we are suffering from. This is why, in the writings of Willie Lynch, the great slave maker who was hired by the American slave masters to teach them how to get maximum usage out of their slaves. In one of Willie Lynch's writings, he has a Warning of Possible Interloping Negatives: he writes, 'the mind has a way of correcting itself when it is left alone and connected to a substantial amount of historical base knowledge.' Willie Lynch is telling the slave masters of America, we must never allow these Negroes to unplug from our system of programming, their mind left alone, and connected to a knowledge of themselves and their God. If we do leave them alone, the original mind will return to the original man, and we will no longer be able to rule him. Unplugging from the slave masters teaching, being in an environment where we are left alone, and plugging into the true source of true historical base knowledge will activate our own self-healing mechanisms of our brain and body as a people. Real historical base knowledge is much deeper than what is taught during Black History Month. During Black History Month we only learn about Black people from the cotton field to the current. From the plantation to the present. We never learn about ourselves before we were slaves. Allah (God) taught the Most Honorable Elijah Muhammad, is the Root Knowledge of our origin in the world.

The electrical energy of the Divine Teachings of the Most Honorable Elijah Muhammad are the jumper cables. This is the source we need to plug into. And when we do plug into that energy we become, what it made the Most Honorable Elijah Muhammad and what it made the Honorable Minister Louis Farrakhan: Powerful, pious, proud, productive, performers, makers of things that happen. Happy, stress free, peaceful, and contented of mind. Whatever we want, we will get it if we make our mind up. If we make our mind up to stay tuned in and plugged into the electrical energy of the of Divine Teachings of the Honorable Elijah Muhammad, we will have the ability to add to the mind what we need and subtract everything that we should not have in it and we will make unlimited progress.

Learn to Use

When a person comes into the ranks of the Nation of Islam, we are blessed to receive **The Supreme Wisdom Lessons**. The *'Lessons'* as we affectionately call them, house formula, that when unpacked allows the student to think supreme thoughts, do supreme deeds and acquire supreme things. NOTE: The Honorable Minister Louis Farrakhan has stated that, "The **Supreme Wisdom** will be of no benefit unless it is married with good morals." It is, by itself, 'potential' energy and is only transferred into 'kinetic' energy when married with this spiritual trait of the possessor. One of the sections in the *Lessons* is called *The Problem Book*.

This Book teaches the Lost- Found Nation of Islam a thorough knowledge of our miserable state of condition in a mathematical way when we were found by OUR SAVIOUR, W. D. FARD. There are 34 problems in the Problem Book, and one of these problems has been extracted by the Saviour and given its own separate page. The problem in the Problem Book that was given its own page is Problem Number 13 which reads,

"After learning Mathematics, which is Islam, and Islam is Mathematics, it stands true. You can always prove it at no limit of time. Then you must learn to use it and secure some benefit while you are living, that is—luxury, money, good homes, and friendship in all walks of life.
Sit yourself in Heaven at once! That is the greatest Desire of your Brother and Teachers.
Now you must speak the Language, so you can use your Mathematical Theology in the proper Term —otherwise you will not be successful, unless you do speak well, for she knows all about you.

NURI MUHAMMAD

The Secretary of Islam offers a reward to the best and neatest worker of this Problem. "

"*After learning Mathematics, which is Islam,* '. Islam is not a religious experience void of logic, Islam is mathematics. This means Islam has logic, reasoning, deduction, and analytical thought processes involved in the establishment of faith. When we were growing up, when we had a question regarding some religious teaching in church, we were told, 'You just gotta have faith.' ' You just gotta believe.' 'God works in mysterious ways.' 'Don't question God.' Wait a minute! Jesus said, in Matthew 7:7, "Ask and it shall be given. Seek, and ye shall find. Knock, and the door shall be open unto you." If we take the first letter of ask, seek and knock, we have **ASK**. So, who said, don't question God?

We wanted to have faith. We wanted to believe. However, a faith and a belief that is not rooted in knowledge is not real faith, it is blind faith. Faith is a tool we can use to achieve in life. A very powerful tool. So powerful, that if we had a very small amount as Jesus said, the size of a mustard seed we could say to the sycamore tree be uprooted. We could say to the mountain be removed and placed there. Jesus goes on to say that anything that we desire with faith it shall be possible. Now, imagine having a powerful tool but being blind! To use the tool effectively, we must be able to see. When we bring our mathematical theology to play, we have the ability to see, so we can use this most powerful tool of faith in a way that that allows us to achieve anything we desire.

"*After learning Mathematics, which is Islam, and Islam is Mathematics, it stands true. You can always prove it at no limit of time. Then you must learn to use it and secure some benefit while you are living.* " This is the first learning is Islam, but there is a second learn here. *"Then you must learn to use it and secure some benefit while you are living.* " Learn to use it, this is the practical application side of faith. We cannot just pray hope and wish, let go and let God, wait on our change to come, we have to bring our mathematical mind to work in a mathematical way. For the apostle James said, faith, without works is dead. From Psychology, we learn of a law that says affirmation without discipline is the beginning of delusion. While affirmation with discipline allows one to work their own miracles. Big Momma used to say it like this, "God helps those who help themselves." In Joshua 1:8, God says, *this book of the law shall not depart out of their mouth, but thou shall meditate there on day and night. That thou may observe it to do, according to all that is written there in.* **And thou shall make thy way prosper, and then you shall have good success.** This verse is teaching us, we should not wait on God to do everything for us, if He created us in His image and likeness, and breathed into us of His own spirit, then He has already given us everything we need to do anything we want!

Problem Number 13 closes with, "**Sit yourself in Heaven at once!**" This sentence actually comes before the description of what heaven looks like, which is **"luxury, money, good homes, and friendship in all walks of life."** Heaven will not be just handed or given to you and I. Allah (God) gives us everything we need inside of us to sit ourselves in heaven at once. At once is an idiom that means immediately and right now. It is time for us to trade in this raggedy broke down, Spooky Theology for the Mathematical Theology. *We then* shall make our way prosper and have good success.

Unpacking Variables

The rulers of When we think of math, rarely do we think of a correlation between mathematics and God. One of the most effective and enduring tools of the enemy is the purposeful creation of deception surrounding the separation of math and God. In fact, this separation is a full area of study in many theological schools around the world. However, when you unpack the variables of both the Bible, and the Holy Qur'an we find that God and the Devil both are using mathematics. The very first page of the Bible in Genesis, God is adding the sun, stars and firmament, man! Jesus told Peter, Satan desires you that he might sift you as wheat (division). Gods' mathematics is always addition and multiplication, and the devils mathematics is always subtraction and division. Then Allah (God) tells us the type of math He wants to see us employ, *be fruitful, multiply, and replenish the earth.* -Genesis 1:28

The Most Honorable Elijah Muhammad was taught by his Teacher, Master Fard Muhammad, that Islam is mathematics and mathematics is Islam. *You can always prove it at no limit of time.* You can always Prove it. Prove it. It is proof that separates spooky theology from a mathematical theology. It is proof that separates Faith from blind faith. In 1Thessolians 5:21 we read, '*Prove all things and holdfast to that which is good.*' This means if we cannot prove it, we cannot call it good, if we cannot call it, we cannot hold fast to it. In the military, when we are commanded to hold fast, it means for us to stay in that place or position. The definition of holdfast is to have a firm grip. The definition of prove is to subject to a test, experiment, comparison, analysis, or the like, to determine quality, amount, or acceptability. The Most Honorable Elijah Muhammad in his monumental book, **"Our Saviour Has Arrived,"** pages 59-74 explains the four areas we should find agreement when we are trying to prove a thing to be true. Those four areas are *Scripture, Nature, Science, and Mathematics.* Any spiritual concept that we are taught, should be verified and verifiable in all four of these areas. If we cannot, this means we can notprove it, and if we cannot prove it, we cannot call it and hold onto it.

Mathematics is logic (rational thought) because it **is** Islam and can be proved in no limit of time. However, when we do a word search in the Holy Qur'an for the word *mathematics*, we will not have any results. Islam **is** mathematics and mathematics **is** Islam and the Holy Qur'an is the book of the Muslims. Yet, the word mathematics cannot be found in the Holy Qur'an. Similarly, a key word search in the Bible for the word mathematics also fails to return positive results.

The word *mathematics* is not in the Holy Qur'an nor in the Bible under m-a-t-h-e-m-a-t-i-c-s. However, mathematics is all throughout the Bible and Holy Qur'an. As mathematics is the structured organization of symbols to tell a story in a way that one could not tell it, without using volumes of words; so, it is with the Bible and Holy Qur'an. Allah (God) has taken the key concepts, the key ideas, the key experiences of life on the inside and outside of the human being and structured them into what are called scriptures.

By deviling into these scriptures, we can use both, the Bible and Holy Qur'an, in a mathematical way and calculate the factual outcomes of numerous circumstances without wasting time looking into each circumstance individually. We can extrapolate, by statistical analysis, the predictable outcome of certain actions, in a given circumstance, and utilize that information to avoid a mistake or error. This then works to empower us to create circumstances that have us "winning" every time. We have the ability and the capacity to create circumstances with predictable stable outcomes with our minds.

In the Holy Qur'an we find it written like this, **"travel the Earth, and study the end of those that have gone before you."** The ends represent their results. Mathematically, this means, all we must do is determine the type of outcome we would like to receive, find those who have achieved that outcome, and do what they did, and we will get what they got! When I was young, with the desire to get out of the streets. One day I was sitting on my porch and a thought came to my mind, "I wonder what the dope fiends were doing when they were my age?' I decided not to serve no one that day and just took a tour of the hood. I went to the trap, liquor store, the alley, and I asked each person I found the same question, "what were you doing when you were my age?" All of them said we were getting money just like you.

It then dawned on me, that if they were doing what I'm doing when they were my age, I'm enroute to be doing what they are doing when I become their age. That gave me adequate motivation to quit that day and never return to that lifestyle.

In all the schools we visit, I tell the young soldiers, do not just interview the people you do not want to be like and ask them what they were doing when they were your age. Interview people that you do want to be like and ask them the same question. What you will find is the people that you want to be like, will tell you what they did that worked. The people you do not want to be like will tell you what they did that did not work and what they wish they would have done. If you can do what they did that worked, eliminate the things that did not work, and replace them with the things that a successful person does and what they wish they had done, you can become them faster than they became themselves! This is mathematics of the mind that allows you to turn decades into days.

The Holy Qur'an says of itself, ***"In this book there are similitudes of every kind."*** Similitude, meaning similarities or similar stories. In this book, there are similar stories of every kind, but we cannot read in the Holy Qur'an about blended families, not as a subject. We do not read in the Holy Qur'an about crack addiction, as a subject. However, if in this book there are similitudes of every kind, this means we can find the cure to crack addiction in the Holy Qur'an. We can find the formula on how to parent in a blended family in the Holy Qur'an. We, in fact, can find every situation and circumstance under some story in the Holy Qur'an, if we can decode the mathematical formula that it is written in.

Mathematically Precise Logical Thoughts

Religion is controlled   Islam, the Honorable Minister Louis Farrakhan teaches, is everything.   Since Islam, is mathematics and mathematics is Islam, then mathematics is everything.   It is the Sun. It is the Moon. It is the Stars. We cannot drive without math. When we see two cars that have collided, this is a sign that the wrong math was used. Too much acceleration resulting in a miscalculation of distance, a violation of the *Law of Mathematics* which then caused a collision.

When boxers are in the ring, one wins, and the other loses. The winner, by analysis, employed mathematics better than the one that lost. The winner calculated the distance between he and his opponent and adjusted to avoid the trajectory of the punch in time to land a counter punch. Winner. Another example, when we get in the shower and turn the knob, two options present themselves hot and cold. Have you ever just haphazardly turned the knob and jumped in, and the water was too hot or too cold? What was wrong? Wrong math. Because mathematics says that a certain number of turns of hot water will render a specific ratio of hot to cold water.

Scientifically, did you know that there are only four colors? Five fragrances? Yet every department store fragrance counter has hundreds of fragrances. Look at all the colors in the world, all derived from four primary colors. Look at all we do in life, everything we do is the result of the organization of a mathematical code through the distribution of five basic senses. These few senses and few colors can be combined in a mathematical sequence where four units of red, two units of blue, one unit of yellow and another few units of white produce a dazzling bouquet of flowers, a rainbow kaleidoscope of nature. *Everything is mathematics.*

When we come into the Nation of Islam, we are given ***Actual Facts***. The recitation of these facts produces mathematically precise logical thoughts. We learn the Law of Cause and Effect. We learn that this law arises from a careful observation of Allah's (God's) creative nature as manifested in the universe. This scientific observation then is the impetus for scientific thought (reasoning). True scientific inquiry then is based not on irrational thinking (spookism) but logical thought in alignment with the Law of Cause and Effect. For every cause, there is an effect. Written as mathematical formula Cause = Effect. As the Honorable Minister Louis Farrakhan teaches us, ***"If the rain is real how then can the cause be unreal?"***

When we look closely at how mathematics is applied in this world, we find it is used as a way of producing artificial confidence, in the predictability of future events, based upon a twisted application of logic. We live in a world that teaches us to take everything to God in prayer and leave it with God but do nothing. Sit and wait for God to do for us what we have asked of Him. When we do this, what we are really doing is making a demand on God, while we absolve ourselves of responsibility. If God does not meet our demand (s), then we can blame God using this as the excuse, to continue without personal correction.

We must understand that we cannot just pray and not work. The Bible teaches in James 2:14 that *"faith without works is dead."* Prophet Muhammad said, *"Mere belief accounts for nothing except that it is carried into practice."* In the world of psychology, there is an axiom that states, *"Affirmation without discipline is the beginning of delusion. While affirmation with discipline allows man to create their own miracles."* Even in the Gospel of Big Mama, (smile). She always said, *God helps those who help themselves.* In most black families, Big Mama said this so much, to keep us from being lazy, and or spooky, that we thought it was a Bible verse! Truth is, it is in the word of God, found in the Holy Qur'an in Surah 13:11. This chapter opens with the protection of Allah (God) and closes with the punishment of Allah (God). This verse 13:11 is right in the middle. Why? Because working it secures Allah's protection and allows the Believer to escape Allah's punishment. It reads, "Surely, *Allah changes, not the condition of a people, until that people change their own condition."*

The Nooridin translation of the Holy Qur'an translates surah 13:11, giving us the formula to change our own condition. It reads, *"Allah changes, not the condition of a people, until that people change their own thoughts and ways."* Thoughts are real. They are unseen, but they are not unreal. I have said this a few times before, you have to become a millionaire long before you ever acquire a million dollars. Millionaire is a mindset, and a million dollars is the reality. This shows us that success or excellence happens twice. First in the mind and second in reality. However, this verse also tells us we cannot just think a thing into existence, "ways" have to change. We must override the self-defeating and self-destructing habits we have and replace them with pious, proud, powerful and productive habits. We are what we repeatedly do. *Excellence is then not an act, but a habit.*

We want a new business. We pray and ask God to give us what we want but the mathematical equation is not balanced. Meaning, we want a business, but we have not cleaned up our credit, written a business plan, done a market analysis, created a budget or timeline for launch. We want our own home but as a renter we do not care for where we are renting as though the rental property is our own. But we demand that God bless us? In the book of Matthew, 25:21, God says *"you were faithful over a few things, now I will make you ruler over much."* To be faithful means to take care of, be dutiful to, to handle with honor. Allah (God) is analyzing us, to see how much care and dutifulness we have for the "few thing" He has already blessed us with, to see if we are qualified to rule the much.

The Most Honorable Elijah Muhammad teaches in the illuminating and monumental book, ***Message to the Black Man,*** an equation for a proper prayer. In the section on prayer, the Most Honorable Elijah Muhammad teaches that our prayer should be primarily, a prayer of Thanksgiving, and then one that petitions. Expressing our deep gratitude to Allah, the Supreme Being, for all of the gifts that He has bestowed on us. Then asking Allah (God), not necessarily for Him to do it or get it for us, but that He will infuse us with His spirit, His energy, His power that we may secure what we are asking for. We should pray that as we go about creating this business plan, striving to get a new home or get in the shape that we could be a good home for His spirit, that He might guide and incline in our life people, situations, circumstances, and events that we can use to achieve the objective.

Mathematics says that after we get His spirit, after we have His energy, after we have summoned His power and we know where to read His word, it is our job, our responsibility, to study, work and remain in a process of continuous self-improvement; until we bring about the results, that we are trying to mathematically work out. We have to be on our Deen (righteous and faithful living) and our grind. Our Beingness times our Doingness will = Our Havingness!

We learn from the above scriptures and facts, that our prayers are not answered according to our faith while we are talking, but they are answered in accordance with our faith while we are working. Note: sometimes we can pray and work properly, and still may not feel as though we achieved the objective. Allah (God) says in the Holy Qur'an chapter 40:60, *"Pray to Me, I will answer you."* He promises to answer our prayers; however, sometimes the answer is "no" or "not right now." This is where patience comes in. What is patience? The ability to work and wait with the right attitude. Something I say and strive to apply when tackling any task is, "Pray like everything depends on God, but work like everything depends on you!"

"The Supreme wisdom will be of no benefit if it is not married to good morals."

-The Honorable Minister Louis Farrakhan

You Are What You Eat

The *Supreme Wisdom* is the core nucleus, the foundation, of the life-giving teachings of the Most Honorable Elijah Muhammad, written in coded language. Why coded language? When we are trying to enter a locked door that has a code, we must know the formula, the proper mathematical sequence to gain access. If we do not know the sequence of numbers needed to open the door, we are denied access. Master Fard Muhammad said that there are 60,000 books of mathematics. The Caucasian only has one book of mathematics, but there are 59,999 left that he did not have access to. Look at all that they have accomplished with just one book. He has become very wise with this one book, Wickedly Wise. The other books had to be hidden from him. If he had access to the other books, we may never be able to get him out of power. You see the Caucasians always digging and diving. They claim they are looking for dinosaur bones, but dinosaurs never existed! They are trying to dig up some of the lost books or the lost knowledge that was hidden from them so they can increase their power and longevity on the planet. Even if they found the books, they would never be able to understand them properly. Their nature will not allow them to work the code to unlock the meaning of the wisdom that they found. What is the code? The Honorable Minister, Louis Farrakhan said, "The Supreme wisdom will be of no benefit if it is not married to good morals.

The code to unlock the power of the *Supreme Wisdom* is righteousness. When we are living other than our own selves, no matter what we do, we are unable to determine the right sequence of numbers to unlock the power found in the wisdom. We are righteous by nature and the more we strive to be upright by overcoming the gravitational pull of this world through righteous thoughts, actions, and deeds plus a righteous physical diet, the more we can tap into and unlock the power of the *Supreme Wisdom*. The beauty of the word of

God, is that the more you feed on it, the more righteous you become. The more knowledge you have on how harmful something bad is for you, the easier it is for you to say no to it when tempted to do the bad. The more knowledge you have on the benefit of something good for you, the easier it is for you to do that good even when you do not feel like doing it.

Gastroenterologists have discovered a scientific fact that, *"you are what you eat."* Notice I use the language; feed on the word of God. In the book of Ezekiel 3:1, God says, *"mortal man, eat of this scroll."* In Matthew 4:4, Jesus says, *"man, cannot live off of bread alone, but every word that proceeded out of the mouth of the Lord."* The prophet Jeremiah says in Jeremiah 15:16, *"your words were found, and I ate them."* All through the scripture, the word of God is called food. Well, the Honorable Minister, Louis Farrakhan teaches us, that for every physical law, there is in the universe its spiritual counterpart. Whatever we eat, we adopt the characteristics of this applies to physical food and the word. This takes the phrase; you are what you eat to another level! When we feed on the **Supreme Wisdom**, we become a supreme being! The Most Honorable Elijah Muhammad said, ***"God has given me a strong and invincible truth. It will Protect you. It will Defend you. It will Prevent you from falling victim to the arch Deceiver."*** When we feed on the invincible truth, we become invincible!

New Math

We must understand that when we are dealing with Supreme Mathematics, we are dealing with a form of mathematics that moves us beyond a simplistic understanding of numbers. Supreme Mathematics deals with the complex science of the mathematical sequencing of the world of the unseen—*the world of what they call the thought matrix*. The Honorable Elijah Muhammad teaches us that when Jesus (Isa) was in school he excelled at mathematics. Jesus (Isa) was so smart that by the age of 12 he had mastered all the known sciences available in public education at that time. In modern terms, he graduated from a PhD level program by the age of 12.

Mr. Yakub did the same thing; however, it took him 18 years. When Mr. Yakub learned all the wisdom in the books available to him in that time, there was nothing left for him to study *outside* of himself. All that was left to study was *inside* of himself. This is how he discovered the brown germ. Mr. Yakub started what we know today as gene splicing through the careful study of DNA, 6,600 years ago. Mr. Yakub was a Blackman and so was Jesus (Isa).

Jesus (Isa), the Honorable Elijah Muhammad teaches us, that he met an old wise man on the way home from school one day. Again, Jesus (Isa) completed school at 12 so when he meets this old wise man, he is not yet 12 years of age. When he met the old wise man, he was coming to teach him Supreme Mathematics. What the Honorable Elijah Muhammad called, the *'radio in the head.'* This means Jesus (Isa) was being taught the science of how to tune in—*the science of thought transmission, receiving and sending.* The Most Honorable Elijah Muhammad said in the ***Theology of Time*** Lecture series, this tuning in is a gift that Allah could give us when we keep ourselves clean inside and out for 20 to 35 years.

Interdependent Entities

"The Brain of Man is Infinite
~The Most Honorable Elijah Muhammad~

Every transmitter is a receiver, and every receiver is a transmitter. For example, a radio in a car does not have wires coming from it connecting it to a pole or directly to a station. Does it? The station transmits the words or music through the wire to the car but if there are no physical wires, what wires are being used? The radio picks up the 'signal' via the airwaves. Meaning, there is a mechanism within the car itself that is so sophisticated it can tune up on a melody and a beat, a frequency, moving through the atmosphere. Then after it tunes *up on*, it can tune *in on*, receive it and then transmit it back to the car. And we can hear the beat, the melody and the words from an airwave (frequency) and have control over the airwave. Whether it is a television, radio, tablet, cell phone, they are a copy of the human brain.

The first wireless internet is not from Microsoft or from Apple. The original computer, the original television, the original radio is in fact the human brain. The devices we use today are cheap replicas of the brain. Therefore, when we see a robot, a radio in a car or a television, these devices are referred to as (AI) artificial intelligence. Just as when we have an orange flavored drink it is in fact artificial or imitation (fake) orange juice. It is a duplicate or a copy of, containing less intrinsic value than the original. Grafted. This means it is less than the original; therefore, the original intelligence is by its nature superior to the artificial intelligence in all aspects. Anything (Ai) can do, (Oi) Original Intelligence, can do even better when the carrier of that intelligence has a clean mind and clean body.

The mind and the body are not independent entities. They are interdependent entities. Which means that they affect each other. The Most Honorable Elijah Muhammad writes on page 31 of *How to Eat to Live Book 1, "There are some people who claim that they do not receive beneficial results as they should. This is due to the wrong mental food that they are eating, which has an effect on their digestive system. To get good results from eating the proper foods, we must have good thoughts. "* The scientists of this world, say, there are only two gates to the human mind, the eyes, and the ears. However, per usual, they are missing a component. There are three gates to the human mind. The eyes, the ears, and the mouth! What you allow through these three gates becomes the raw material that makes what your mind is. When we have a clean mind and a clean body, we can manifest the highest form of mathematics.

The highest form of mathematics is not adding together numbers to make a product. It is adding ideas together to produce a desired result. When you unpack the variables of the scripture, you will find that God's mathematics is always addition and multiplication, and the devils mathematics is always subtraction and division. The basic instructions, God gave to man in the beginning, was, be fruitful, multiply, replenish the earth and subdue it. Mathematics! Multiply is physical reproduction. But that first instruction, be fruitful is spiritual and mental reproduction.

Why was Jesus taught the high science of the *'radio in the head'*? The Bible says in the book of Matthew 9:4, *"And Jesus knowing their thoughts said, Wherefore think ye evil in your hearts?"* Jesus was able to maneuver and avoid the plots of his enemies because he knew what his enemy was thinking. Even greater still, look at what he was able to do when he married the power of his thought with Sound called words. Jesus made 1900 statements. Spoke on 200 subjects. Said 171 things about himself. Issued 131 Commandments. Gave his disciples 41 missions. Performed 40 miracles. All of the miracles, except for one, had nothing to do with "hand laying," he told them something and their healing came from the word (thought, married with sound). Jesus said *"be ye perfect even as your father in heaven, art perfect. I've gone to prepare a place for you that where I am you may also be."* Paul said *"let this mind be in you, the same mind that was in Christ Jesus."* Well, if as a man think of his heart, so is he, and we are being invited to have the same mind as Christ, which is the mind of God, what does that make us? If Jesus is going to prepare a place for us, that where he is, we may also be, that means he has invited us to be on the same level of mental and spiritual power that he operates from. We too can tune in! We too can heal!

The most complicated form of mathematics is not calculus or quantum physics, unless we define quantum physics by its true definition, not by what this world offers as a definition. The word quantum means, by its original (true) definition, ***thought***. The 'physics' or the 'anatomy 'of thought is the highest form of math. Which explains why the two most difficult things to do in life are to listen to other people speak and to pull people together in unity. This is hard, because there are different ideas, different minds, different thought waves or frequencies that must be brought into harmony and in some cases, submission to the superior thought or idea.

The question is, how then can we successfully resolve this level of mathematical problem? By what calculations can we truly solve it? 2 Corinthians 10:5 says, *"bring every thought captive under Christ."* Any thought we think from wherever it came from must be arrested and compare it to the mind of God. if it matches what God has said on that, given subject, keep the thought, but if it does not match, we must kill the thought. This practice of mental mathematics ultimately lands us at being possessors of the mind of God. The scripture says, *"my sheep know my voice a stranger they will not follow,"* so we must stay consistently downloading into our mind "thus saith the Lord statements." by way of scripture and the teachings of the Most Honorable Elijah Muhammad. We then will learn the language of God and know what to accept and what to reject. This is the mathematics of what is called "the spirit of discernment."

Material Witnesses

Again, The Most Honorable Elijah Muhammad teaches that we cannot learn how to tune in. He said this is a *gift* from Allah (God). However, if we clean ourselves up, inside and out and then Allah (God) *may* grant us the gift of the *radio in the head*. This is powerful. Why did Jesus say in Matthew 18:20, *"Wherever there are two or more gathered together in my name, there I am also."* Jesus is not present. Right? Yet, his mind is still present.

On one occasion, the Honorable Elijah Muhammad was asked a question about angels, he said, ***"There are no such things as angels that are moving around in the atmosphere. The only thing moving around in the atmosphere are righteous thoughts."*** The basic functionality of a radio is that it tunes up on and tunes in on an airwaves, a frequency, in order to both receive and transmit the signal. The human brain can also tune up on the brains, the minds, of the righteous; by accessing the thoughts of the wise, the thoughts of the powerful, as they move through the atmosphere. This is not spooky. This **is** mathematics.

Allah (God) gives people gifts, and He is the best giver of gifts. What is a gift? A gift is the successful mastery of a skill or set of skills that someone possesses, a skill that they may have done nothing to earn. There are individuals, gifted by Allah (God) with the capacity to master mathematical formulas enabling them to use telepathy, clairvoyance, clairaudience and numerous other skills. Why does Allah (God) give these types of gifts? He gives these gifts so these individuals can be a witness to human potential.

If there were no material witnesses to human potential, and only what was on paper was to be taken as evidence of what could and could not be accomplished, nobody would believe greater could be achieved. For example, before Roger Bannister ran the mile in under 4 minutes, it was believed that it could not be done. Roger Bannister ran the 4-minute mile in 1954 in 3:59:04. Within three months of Roger Bannister, breaking the four-minute mile, another man did. A few months later they were 12 men and that had broken the four-minute mile. Now there are hundreds who have. There's an old saying, that you cannot be what you do not see. You can be what you do not see, it just makes it much easier when your mind knows someone else has done it. Your spiritual peripheral vision gets turned on, and you say to yourself, if they can do it, so can I!

On July 7, 1999, Hicham El Guerrouj, from Morocco, ran the 4-minute mile in 3:43:13. This means whatever we read about of human power to manifest in the spiritual realm, we can do greater than that today. John 14:12, Jesus says, *"Verily, verily, I say, unto you, he that believeth on me, the works that I do shall he do also; and greater works than these shall he do;* Scripture says you judge a tree by the fruit bears, and a man by his works. If Jesus is telling us that we can do greater works, he wants us not just to become like him, but to be even greater than him.

By Allah (God) granting these gifts to people, to individuals of His choice, what they accomplish becomes a bearer of witness to human potential—the God within. How do we know these giftings exist? Again, because we have historical records of real people who have received these giftings that we can use to verify these things as actual facts.

A study by Duke University published in *Harper's Magazine,* marks the first time an article has ever been written where a serious study was conducted into human potential. Roughly, 100,000 different tests were performed on thousands of people. As an aspect of the test, the researchers asked the participants to correctly identify as many cards as possible. They had to use cards from a specially prepared deck of cards, without using any type of sensory function cues; meaning they could not look at the cards (see them) nor touch them (tactile). Some of the participants were in the same location but others were geographically dispersed. The results showed that a large group of these people could correctly identify a significant number of the cards. Meaning, they could identify cards that they had never seen or touched before.

A result of the study was that the researchers were able to conclude, that the faculty of mind, which allowed the study participants to 'read' the cards correctly, is the same faculty of mind that allows telepathic and clairvoyant information to enter the mind. What was identified is that this is a higher, more refined sensory function, which enables sight, without the use of the physical eyes. This 'extra-sensory' function has been called many things over the years. The sixth sense and the third eye are two of the more commonly used names. *This is the real power of our mind, to travel through space and time without the physical body.*

To one degree or another every person has had an experience with this extra-sensory response. For example, have you ever been somewhere and said, *'I've been here before?'* Have you ever heard somebody say something and you knew exactly what they were going to say *before* they said it? How? In French, they call these experiences, *de ja vu*. It is simply the power of the mind to move through space and time without the body. These experiences are a glimpse into the capacity of the mind to perform infinite calculations, using supreme mathematics.

While this extra sensory experience was documented by this study, what they could not provide was a specific regiment, or mental exercise routine for the brain. A routine any person could do to develop this skill. Again, this is a gift directly from Allah (God) and while we cannot demand that Allah (God) give it to us, we can prepare ourselves and become excellent candidates, to receive it through righteousness and disciple.

Prepared to Receive a Gift

These researchers could not identify a routine; however, The Honorable Elijah Muhammad has given us the perfect routine. The routine is simple: Clean ourselves up **inside** and **out**. What is the definition of internal cleansing? What does it mean to be clean on the outside? We cannot have a disorganized environment and expect to have organized thoughts. We cannot live in a dirty environment and have clean thinking. The environment that we live in, the space that we govern or control, where we are the god's of, the space must be clean and organized. The cleaner and more organized it is the easier it is for us to maintain a consistent level of refined thought process. Cleanliness is so powerful that when you clean your car inside and out, the car even runs better! (Smile) Well, it doesn't, but this shows the great psychological impact cleanliness has on the mind.

Many of us when we were growing up, we heard repeatedly, cleanliness is next to Godliness. Well, that's close. The Honorable Minister Louis Farrakhan said, *"Cleanliness is not next to Godliness, cleanliness is Godliness!"* Clean *inside* and *out*. The Honorable Minister Louis Farrakhan made this profound statement in **The Time and What Must Be Done** lecture series, *"You are what you eat, and even more what you think."* This clean inside and out process starts with regulating what goes in our minds and our mouths. Dear brothers and sisters, we must remember that all food, physical and mental, is one of two things. It's either Tonic or Toxic. Toxic is that which depresses and weakens. Tonic is that which invigorates and strengthens. Tonic thoughts: *"Finally, brothers, whatever is true, whatever is honorable, whatever is just, whatever is pure, whatever is lovely, whatever is commendable, if there is any excellence, if there is anything worthy of praise, think about these things." -Philippians 4:8*

Tonic Food: Navy Beans, Whole Milk, Vegetables, Fruit, and Whole Wheat Bread. (Complete list and way to consume found in *How To Eat To Live Book 1&2* by The Most Honorable Elijah Muhammad)

The researchers also concluded that when people come together in a sincere and righteous way, with the goal of solving problems, they can tap into this power. And, as a collective, they can discern and define solutions to any problem put before them. Verifying what Jesus said, When there are two or more of you gathered in My name, there I am in the midst of thee. (Matthew 18:20). Righteous people coming together for righteous things gives us access to Christ Consciousness, the Mind of Muhammad, and Allah Awareness!

The researchers call this atmosphere, the *ether*. They concluded that the ether is a form of energy moving at an extremely high rate of vibration. The ether is filled with a form of universal power. This power, this energy, adapts itself to the nature of the predominate thoughts that we as individuals and as a collective hold in our mind. This power, this energy then influences us in supernatural ways. This allows us to transmit and transmute our thoughts into their physical equivalent. This is all real. This is all science. This is all Supreme Mathematics. The problem is this power, this energy does not discriminate. We can be in the world but not of the world. The Most Honorable Elijah, Muhammad said, *"The hereafter for my followers is now."* He did not qualify the statement with "when the white man's power is broken, or "when there's no more evil on the planet." We can live in an environment that is Hell, and still operate in a personal heaven.

In the book of Malachi 4:6, the last days are called the *"great and dreadful day of the Lord."* Two opposite extremes, existing at the same time in one environment could only take place if different people are experiencing different realities. It is great for some, and dreadful for others! Strong, righteous, positive thoughts will help us to bring heaven into our lives, families, and communities. Weak, unrighteous, negative thoughts will help us to bring hell into our lives, families, and communities.

Being Turned

In the world of sports, there are two oft repeated mantras, "you will play like you practice" and "practice makes perfect." The problem is these sayings are not true. The reality is perfect practice makes perfect. When a person consistently organizes their time and disciplines themselves—physically and mentally, but they are practicing in the wrong manner, what happens is the person just becomes proficient at doing things the wrong way. So perfect practice makes perfect.

To be successful in a team sport, everyone must maintain their individuality while learning to lend their skills and talents to the whole, so everyone wins. When you play on a basketball team, sometimes the coach will have the entire team shooting free throws. Why? Because one person missed their free throw in the game. The coach will have the whole team running bleachers. Why? Why must everyone run the bleachers and shoot free throws? In the game, if some of the players make mistakes, the whole team suffers. Suffering as a team for an individual mistake is the way it is in a real game.

The coach understands the "collective suffering of the team" fosters unity among the team and destroys rugged individualism, envy, and jealousy. When a close game goes to overtime the team members who do not want to run any extra suicides or bleachers in the next practice, begins cheering on any player that they know struggles with their free throws long before they have to take the shot. Let them hit their free-throw, the whole team goes crazy in a positive way celebrating. Now the coach knows, after all they have been through in practice, if they can play like they practice, no player will lose their individual gifted shine and they will be a great team.

This analogy holds true when we are seeking Allah (God) for understanding. Allah (God) is the Master Coach of every divine servant who is committed to His assignment. Allah (God) wants to know whether your prayer, your sacrifice, your life, and your death are all for Him. Allah (God) says in The Holy Qur'an 29:1, *"Do men think that they will be left alone, saying, they believe, and will not be tried? When truly, we tried those before that Allah may know the truthful ones from the liars."* The Honorable Minister Louis Farrakhan teaches us that it is not that Allah (God) needs to know whether we are truthful or liars. He already knows this; it is the God *within* that needs to know. So, all mighty Allah (God) uses what we may deem to be undeserved suffering or unearned trials to show us our own authenticity as a Believer.

Allah (God) tries us with something of fear, hunger, loss of property, loss of life, diminution of fruit or loss of money, being lied on, with false accusations, with being arrested, being imprisoned. He tries us with betrayal by our friends and our very own family. In the Holy Qur'an He tries us to make manifest what we are made of—not to Him because He already knows who we are, He wants us to see ourselves in truth. So that one day, when we are in a real battle, when it is you and the beast, you and Goliath, you and the arch deceiver, you and the great wonder in heaven called dragon, you will smile and remember the lies and the false accusations. Remember the hours spent studying, the physical exercises, the discipline, the focus, and Allah (God) will bless us with the ability to defeat our enemy based on our training. *The real weapon of a man or woman of God is their believing mind.*

When we go through tests and trials that we feel are undeserved, it forces us to pray earnestly seeking a logical explanation for what we are going through, because those around us are unable to

explain why we are going through hell. What we must understand is
that Allah (God) uses circumstances and situations as training grounds
to turn average people into masters of those circumstances. To master
the circumstances, we must *master our thinking*. We as Muslims say,
"Oh Allah, Surely, I have turned myself to Thee. " Sometimes we do
turn ourselves to Allah and sometimes **we are turned** to Allah. The
Honorable Minister Louis Farrakhan teaches us that we could say,
"Surely I am being turned" because when we get lied on, we get turned
to Allah (God). When we go through trials and difficulties, the loss of
property, diminution of fruit, fear, hunger, domestic problems, we are
turned by those circumstances to Allah, to God, being upright, to Him
who originated us. We do not want to talk to anyone else. We want to
talk to Allah (God) the originator of the Heavens and the Earth;
because we know for sure that He understands.

We say to the Originator, **"Surely my prayers, my sacrifice,
my life and my death are all for Allah, the Lord of the Worlds. "** In
that divine order, we cannot die for that which we will not live for,
and we cannot live for that which we will not sacrifice for. We cannot
sacrifice for what we have not even prayed for. Prayer provides us
with the proper *orientation of mind* for the next level of development
called *sacrifice*. Sacrifice prepares us for the *proper orientation* of the
mind for another level called *Living for the Cause*. And Living for the
Cause prepares our mind for the *proper orientation* of dying for what
we believe in. But we cannot pray and then die. We cannot sacrifice
and then die. We must pray and then sacrifice, sacrifice, and then live,
live and then give our life as a living sacrifice to that which we believe
in.

The Difficulty Factor

The Honorable Minister Louis Farrakhan teaches, "everything of value has…" look at this, not by it or around it but within it, an inherent *"difficulty factor"*. When something is inherent, this means it comes with it and if it is inside of it, it is not attached to it and separated from it, it is the internal ingredients of it. So, if everything of value has built into it, not something from somewhere else but as a part of its own intrinsic nature, difficulty, then surely, we must go through and master difficulties repeatedly. Facing difficulty, mathematically recalculating our stratagems. Employing these recalculated stratagems at the appropriate time and in the appropriate measure, when we encounter difficulties, as we move toward our goals and objectives will lead to success.

The Honorable Minister Louis Farrakhan further teaches, *"whether it is the lowest form of insect or man himself, we see that overcoming adversity is necessary part of life"*. Look at the mathematics of what the Honorable Minister Louis Farrakhan is explaining. Since life cannot come into existence without difficulty, the very fact that life itself cannot come into existence without difficulty demonstrates that difficulty is a mandatory part of remaining in existence.

The Honorable Minister Louis Farrakhan in the message titled, *"The Swan Song"* stated, *"You were made to conquer whatever life presents."* You did it as sperm, why do you think you can't do it now. He went on to say that the Most Honorable Elijah Muhammad told us that there were three trials that we had to go through to come into existence, and we have to overcome the same three trials to remain in existence, alive.

1. Surviving in a hostile environment

2. Gravity

3. Competition

It is a natural law that whatever you do to get a thing, you must keep doing to keep that thing. When the sperm enters the vaginal tract that sperm must face difficulty. There were three-hundred million other sperm in competition to seek out and reach the one egg. Three-hundred million of them in a trial, struggling, all of them with the same goal, but only one will reach the egg and achieve the goal.

The vaginal tract is the first difficulty factor that we face. The sperm is faced with intense competition as it tries to reach the egg first. The white blood cells in the body, whose function is to fight bacteria, perceives the sperm as a threat and goes to war trying to kill the sperm. All of this is taking place while the sperm is swimming upstream, *against* gravity. Three levels of difficulty for the sperm alone. Once the sperm reaches the egg, this mix of sperm and ovum produces the clot. The clot then goes through a unique level of difficulty to become the embryo. The embryo goes through several months of difficulty to become a fetus.

Then one day, the water breaks. The warm and secure environment the fetus has grown comfortable in is now destroyed. Difficulty. Discomfort. Pain. The mother must push because the baby is coming—all options are gone. When the baby comes, we see bruising on the shoulders, sometimes disfigurement of the head. Baby crying because it just successfully finished nine months of difficulty. Well, if the baby adapted and successfully handled all these difficulties, on all these levels, to come into existence, to earn this thing called life. Then what would make us think, that as a full-grown man or woman, that we would not have to deal with multiple difficulty factors, in the time that we live on this planet?

Successfully overcoming any difficulties requires absolute determination. There are no witnesses at 3AM when you are working on yourself, working on your dream, or your craft. It is you and Allah (God). You and your dream. When doors close and friends abandon you, family members question you. The person you have given your heart to doubts you and walks away from you. No witnesses, no cheer squad. Just you and the grind. It is in these moments we must remain humble and hungry, and *"seek assistance through patience and prayer"* (Holy Qur'an 2:45). Which will allow us to come through it and remain on the upper trajectory toward our oneness with Allah (God).

It is imperative that we embrace the grind. That we be journey happy, not destination happy. That we enjoy the process not just the product. When we become to destination, happy or product oriented, we can become frustrated with what we deem is "taking too long." The Honorable Minister Louis Farrakhan calls this the sin of ignorance. The sin of ignorance is, "the disappointment in the "apparent" slowness of Allah's reward for faithful service." You must always remember that Allah is not a judge, but He is the Master of the Day of Judgment. This means that Allah manifests perfect execution of the law of reciprocity. With Allah, you cannot calculate growth or reward on a traditional corporate America time clock or calendar.

We must study nature to understand Allah's (God's) clock. In nature, there is an object called the Chinese bamboo tree. A Chinese bamboo tree takes five years to grow. It must be watered and fertilized in the ground where it has been planted every day. It does not break through the ground for five years. You must consistently water the bamboo tree, even though you cannot see any growth. If you miss a few days, you have to start the five-year cycle all over again. You must keep feeding it, keep watering it even when you do not see any sign of progress. The Holy Qur'an says that there is a message in creation for those who believe. What a message we see in the Chinese bamboo. The Chinese bamboo tree takes five years just to break the ground. But once it breaks through the ground, it will grow 90 feet tall in five weeks! Sometimes progress and growth are the same. We may have many years of watering and working, and all of the sudden, we see 100 fold growth in five weeks!

Well Defined Desire

Successful men and women, no matter the field of endeavor, when we study them, we learn that all of them have one thread of commonality. A thread of commonality that unites them no matter the ethnic background, socio-economic status, no matter the field of endeavor—a single common thread. That thread of commonality is a well-defined and well-developed singular desire—aim, purpose, goal to which they turn themselves. A singular goal. This goal produces what many call a burning desire, 'insane focus,' or a 'magnificent obsession' for the achievement of that which they are striving for. No matter what field of human endeavor you are looking in, **wherever success is, sacrifice was.**

Every successful person was willing to pay their dues. When we read about these individuals the questions are always, *'How did you become so great at.... or make your company so...?'* The answer usually goes, *'I had to give up everything and go all in...I started off selling cassette tapes out of the trunk of my car...I practiced every moment I got...I skipped hanging out with friends...I studied at lunch and on every break...I studied on the bus and the train....There were days when I didn't know where I was gonna sleep, where I was gonna get my next meal.'* This same story can be found in the autobiography of every great one, male or female. They all were radically focused; they all had a magnificent obsession. They all had a burning desire.

The question is, is it possible that we could have radical focus, a magnificent obsession, a burning desire about something that is not right or righteous? Committing ourselves 100% to the achievement of something but wind-up losing self, our very soul, in the process? Clearly, if we are determined, we must be determined about the *right thing* for the *right reason*. Success is not an act. It is a habit. This means a consistent doing of a thing. We are what we repeatedly do. To be successful, we must have a campaign of discipline to achieve the objective. The Honorable Minister Louis Farrakhan said this, ***"the more sincere the motive, the more sustained the action.***

Allah (God) makes it clear, in the Holy Qur'an, that without determination we will not have anything. The Holy Qur'an 53:39 states, ***"Man shall have nothing, but that which he strives for."*** To strive, is a combination of trying and struggling ***simultaneously***. Trying to achieve something that we are focused on, or obsessed over, ignites the fire of desire to achieve that which we are seeking.

While we are striving to succeed, dues must be paid, because again, everything of value has a difficulty factor attached to it. When difficulties manifest themselves, this is not to be taken as a sign that whatever the endeavor is, is wrong. If what we are doing, does not violate the laws of God, nor the rights of our fellow man, revealing of the difficulty factor is taken as a sign that the correct course *is* being followed. So, if we are striving and we can have nothing but what we strive for, we cannot make a half-hearted attempt or try and be successful. We must attempt or try and then meet and overcome all obstacles in our path. As we read in Colossians 3:23, *"Whatever you do, work at it with All Your Heart, as working for the Lord, not for men."*

Note: If you are having problems staying motivated, stay consistent. Your consistency will give you back your motivation!

During this arduous process, Allah (God) comforts the Believer. In the Holy Qur'an 84:6, Allah (God) tells us ***"And soon you shall see the ends for which men strive."*** Yes, we must try. Yes, we are going to make an attempt. Yes, it is going to be hard. Yes, it will be difficult. Yes, there will be a mighty struggle. And yes, we will have to pay our dues, but not forever. Soon we shall see the ends for which men strive.

Think of it this way, in order to be just a basic level Believer, the Holy Qur'an 30:30 says, *"...Set thy face for religion, being upright, the nature made by Allah in which He has created man."* This teaches us, that before we can even be a regular basic level believing person, we have to have some amount of determination.

When a person competes in a track meet, they receive three commands. On your mark or get ready. Get set? Go. Prior to the start of the race, the announcer says get set, the athlete is loose, smiling, playing around, joking, dancing. But as soon as the command on your mark comes that same person is no longer thinking about the crowd or anything trivial. They are focused on the finish line. They have their mind geared up for whatever amount of distance they must successfully cross to win. That person has made a personal commitment that no matter what happens I am going to give my all for this pocket of time! When that gun goes off, they have their mind fixed on not just doing good but doing the absolute best they humanely can. They are not trying to just compete; they are striving to beat everybody on the line.

To be successful, we must get focused. We must be determined, have a magnificent obsession, a burning desire, and an insane focus to be what our nature has demanded of us to be; and that is righteous. Understand that we are righteous by nature; everything else we are or have become, is by circumstance. This becomes easier when we see ourselves the way, God sees us, and when we live our lives to be pleasing to Allah (God). In the holy Quran, it is repeated several times that the believer takes on a Allah's Colour or Allah's perception.

As the original man and the original woman of the planet, we have to tell ourselves, "I will not allow myself image or any other perception to be shaped by non-scriptural concepts."

In other words, whatever a lot of God has said about me in the scripture, and in the teachings of the Most Honorable Elijah, Muhammad is what I will think of myself. Once this type of mathematics is done, and we began to add up all that God had done. God has said regarding the greatness of man, this becomes a mental impossibility to operate in poor self-worth, low self-esteem, self-doubt, disbelief in your ability to do, to be depressed, or feel less than. If we are in the image and the likeness of God, this means when God looks at us, He sees himself. Our problem is when we look at ourselves. We do not see God! If we are in the image and likeness of God, this means that everything that is true about God is also true about us.

Genesis 1:26, does not just say image, but likeness. The image is of physical reflection. Likeness is a spiritual reflection. Image is the outside. Likenesses are on the inside. In a lecture, called entitled the *Mind of God*, The Honorable Minister Louis Farrakhan explains, likeness means, we are created with the same thought. Mind spirit, nature, quality, and characteristics of God. This means that all of the 99 attributes of Allah (God) are also human characteristics within us. So, all through the Holy Qur'an and in the Bible, we read about what God has done and can do and then we read about this group of people called the We and Us that are allowed to do the same things. Holy Qur'an 2:117, *"When Allah deems a thing, He simply says to it be and it is."* Then in the Holy Qur'an 16:40, *"and when We deem a thing, we simply say to it, be and it is.*" In the Bible, when we see this group called us or in the Holy Qur'an this group called we, it is always a capital W in 'We' and a capital U in 'Us'. When we see the capital, this is not just a cluster of people with people; this is a cluster of people with God. When we operate with a sincere righteous and a pure "why" or motive toward a righteous endeavor, God is with Us, and we can do anything as a group that we have read God did as an individual.

Bidirectional Communication

The world we live in calls an entertainer, a rapper or a singer, an artist. Question. If they are artists, where is the canvas? The canvas is the minds of the people. An artist draws a picture on a canvas. An entertainer draws a picture on the mind!

The subconscious level of the mind never rests, it is always active. The subconscious mind works 24 hours a day, 7 days a week to bring into existence the material and physical reality that perfectly matches the dominant image in the brain. That dominant image is shaped by what we feed the mind the most. **Whatever we feed the mind the most is what wins.** Remember, as we stated in previous chapters, the Most Honorable Elijah Muhammad teaches we had two digestive systems. One in the stomach and one in the brain, and that is why they call it on social media looking at your 'feed.' The Honorable Minister Louis Farrakhan teaches that you are what you eat, and even more what you think. These two digestive systems, the brain and the belly are interdependent entities, with bidirectional communication. What we eat affects what we think and what we think effects what we eat.

The two natures of physical and spiritual food are either one tonic or the other toxic. If we eat, tonic food, but think toxic thoughts, we can override the benefit of the tonic food and vice versa. We must protect these three Gates that lead to our mind. For whatever we allow through these three gates, the eyes, the ears and the mouth, will give us the raw material that we will use to make and build our minds. We should spend much less time on Facebook, and more time in our Faith-Book. For if the majority of what we allow through these three gates is gossip, or what some entertainer said or did, then the image, that the artist has painted on the canvas of the mind; even while we are working, sleeping, worshipping, or praying, the subconscious mind is working tirelessly to bring into existence what someone else has painted on our brain.

The majority of what we see on social media, or in music is negative, degrading, immoral, disrespectful of each other in general and our women in specific. In scripture everything negative and immoral is considered darkness. If someone asked us to paint a picture of happiness, we would use an array of bright, vibrant colors. If someone asked us to paint a picture of sadness or unhappiness, we would use dark gloomy colors. If the lyrics and the social media feed is negative and immoral, we are painting a picture on our minds of sadness and unhappiness. Remember, my dear reader, that **our life is our mind turned inside out.** If the mind's picture is bleak, painted with darkness and gloomy colors, then our life has no choice but to reflect it. In the Bible we read, in Philippians 4:8 *"Finally, brethren, whatsoever things are true, whatsoever things are honest, whatsoever things are just, whatsoever things are pure, whatsoever things are lovely, whatsoever things are of good report; if there be any virtue, and if there be any praise, think on these things."*

We are good people; we just have bad habits. We are righteous by nature and other than that by circumstance. What does it mean when we say something is a thing by nature? This means, a fish born by nature to live in water is more at peace when it is functioning in accord with its nature. When you take that fish out of the water, you see it begin to act differently. Why, because it is in an environment that is not conducive to its nature. Ultimately, if we keep the fish out of water long enough, it will die. Well, man is superior to the fish so man, when taken out of his nature will act crazy; he will not physically die like the fish, but he will spiritually die. Making us the living depiction of the 'walking dead'.

How do we know righteousness is our nature? The Honorable Minister Louis Farrakhan explained, righteousness does not have to be taught. We know it innately; right from wrong. We come to, parents, we come to institutions of religion, the mosque, to be what? Trained. To be given more evidence that we can use to help ward off the inclination to be or do wrong and to give us the justification for being right. The more evidence we have on why something is good, the easier it is to do it. Simple mathematics. Nobody has to teach us; it is natural to be right. It is unnatural to be wrong.

The Holy Qur'an goes on to explain, *"There is no altering Allah's creation."* Meaning, at our core, right now, even after 400 plus years of slavery, suffering and death, 6,000 years of being under the rule of Satan, 50,000 years of living in the jungles of Africa, 66 trillion years of being absent the true knowledge of God, there is still at the very essence of us, righteousness.

Our nature must be nurtured. In science, there is a conflict, where the argument is centered around, is it nature or is it by means of nurture that people become who and what they are? The truth of the matter is, it is both nature and nurture. It is the nurturing of the 'nature', the feeding of the nature that allows us to become. As the Honorable Minister Louis Farrakhan has explained, *"Your nature is correct. You just need to have your nature fed properly with truth, and you will grow in accord with your nature; grow in uprightness."*

Once we have our mind made up, we will find that all the little struggles that we are wrestling with and straddling the fence about, all these excuses, will be eliminated. We will be on the starting block, not thinking about the crowd. All we are thinking about is competing, doing our best and winning by crossing the finish line. This is the level of determination that we not only need but must have. The radical focus, the magnificent obsession. A burning desire for God and His truth, this is when things become easier, and when we are able to achieve maximum development.

Recalibrated Mind

We live in a magnificent universe. We live in a universe of nine planets with one Sun. The Sun is functioning in the way that Allah (God) ordained it to function without any deviation. The Sun is 853,000 miles in diameter, 93,000,000 miles from the planet Earth, registering a consistent temperature of 14,072 degrees. Light travels from the Sun at 186,000 miles per second, which means, every 8 minutes and 20 seconds, a new fresh ray of light (sunshine) comes from the Sun and strikes the Earth's equator. When it strikes the Earth's equator, it causes this great mass of Earth and water totaling 196,940,000 square miles, weighing 6 sextillion tons, (a unit followed by 21 ciphers) to make motion. Despite the Earth's size, that ray of light, from the Sun, traveling that great distance, when it touches the equator, it causes the Earth to begin to rotate. Rotate on its own axis at 1,037 1/3 miles per hour. Meaning, that every 23 hours, 56 minutes and 46 seconds, the Earth makes one complete rotation on its own axis. Every 365 1/4 days, the Earth makes a full revolution around the Sun. Four times a year, the Earth moves a little closer or farther away, giving us summer, spring, winter, and fall.

In this solar system, there are nine planets, and though they are different distances from the Sun, Pluto for example is 4,600,000,000 miles away from the Sun, all the planets travel at the same rate of speed, 1,037 1/3 miles per hour. This speed is constant and happens because the Sun's light hits each planet at their equator which causes them to rotate. The Sun, in its relationship to and in its role in the universe, mimics or copies the power of the mind. Just as we have a Sun and nine planets, we have a mind and nine systems of the body. (integumentary system, the musculoskeletal system, the respiratory system, the circulatory system, the digestive system, the excretory system, the nervous system, the endocrine system, and the reproductive system.). The Sun works within the nature in which Allah (God) created it to do, all the planets are rotating perfectly, in obedience to their divine mandate without objection.

The reality is that if the mind of the black man and woman, is recalibrated to live in harmony with the law of light, then all nine systems of our bodies would work perfectly allowing us to heal from every problem we are suffering from right now. What is this law of light? In the scripture, knowledge is called light, truth is called light, wisdom is called light. David, the Psalmist said, *"the law is the lamp onto my feet."* We describe the comprehension as 'the light of understanding.' Therefore, living in a court with the law of light means that we are in submission to knowledge, wisdom, truth, understanding, and the law of God. Our mind then becomes the Sun of our universe, and then all nine systems of our body work perfectly, allowing us to heal every problem we are have.

The social scientists of this world have conducted numerous studies on the human brain. Many of these studies have focused on the effects of lies on the brain. Bearing witness to what the Honorable Minister Louis Farrakhan teaches us from the Honorable Elijah Muhammad, that the brain cells are created to think right. Right, in this context is not only denoting morally correct standards, but also direction. If something is moving to the right, it is moving in one direction.

We have inside our brains, 14 billion brain cells. Thought travels around those 14 billion brain cells in the right direction at the rate of 24 billion miles per second. The Honorable Elijah Muhammad teaches us that lies go against the *grain* of the brain. Meaning, when we insert a lie into the brain, it goes against the grain and turns the brain's thinking in the opposite direction. Again, let us return to the example of the car, if we were driving a car on the highway and it is in drive, but we continue to slam it in reverse, this act will eventually destroy the engines transmission. The transmission is the device in the car that tells the car which gear to be in, to maintain the proper speed and motion, while driving.

In the human vehicle the brain is the transmission. A car on the expressway maybe going at 65 mph. Our thoughts are not 'driving; at 65 miles per hour. Our thoughts are moving on the *average* of 24 billion miles per second. Therefore, if lies continue to be inserted into the brain, then our transmission, our ability to transfer and transmit ideas into reality, is severely damaged, if not destroyed. Our ability to successfully navigate from where we are to where we are trying to go, at the rate we set out to is dramatically slowed, producing frustration and anger. Frustration and anger being defined as incoherent thought processes, which produce verbally and occasionally physically violent outbursts.

In a book entitled, *Psyche Wars*, author Del Jones, mentions that the most damaging and destructive lie ever inserted into the psyche of Black men and women is the lie that Jesus was a white man. Why is the question of Jesus' true skin color such a damaging thought to engage? In the human brain, there are logic circuits. Logic circuits allow a person to mathematically, logically compute, sort and store incoming information. The effect of telling the lie, that Jesus is white, reorients the mind in the following manner: *'Jesus is white. Jesus is the son of God. If Jesus is the son of God and he is white, then Jesus' father, God, must be white too. If God is good, if God is love and I am black. I am the opposite of white, which means I am the opposite of good and love. I am the opposite of God.'* While we do not say these things to ourselves on a conscious level, on a subconscious, subliminal level, we have been saying this to ourselves for the last 400 plus years.

This is why we gang bang, drug deal and misuse and abuse one another.

We use sport and play, participating in games or watching entertainment, as a *coping mechanism*. A coping mechanism which allows us the opportunity to take a mental break from 'hell 'though we know, the relief we find, is only temporary. The hope that we found in the moment does not and can never fully satisfy or solve any of the problems we face. None of these activities places us in a state of permanent happiness, joy or heaven right here on Earth, in the now.

For any of us to fully realize our potential, we must have a plan. We must have, for the lack of a better word, a playbook. A playbook is a plan, an outline that features a well thought out and thought through set of actionable strategies. Where we find any person or group that is successful, particularly over a long period of time, without fail, it is because they had and have a plan.

Mindset

The first book from the Most Honorable Elijah Muhammad is entitled, ***Message to the Black Man in America.*** In ***Message to the Black Man***, the Most Honorable Elijah Muhammad does not mention planning anything until page 129. He makes note of what Satan is planning to do on a few occasions, but he does not mention that *we* should be planning anything until page 129. The question is, *"Why would the Most Honorable Elijah Muhammad wait that late in the book to start introducing the fact that we must have a plan, if a plan is the only means of being successful?"* The reality is, for us to create an actionable plan, we must have the proper ***mindset***.

Mindset: the right orientation of mind, perception of self and a worthy goal. When someone does not know who they are, how great they are, how much power they have, it is a clear indicator that they do not see their reflection properly, when they look in the mirror of their own human potential. The goals that they come up with when they are blind to their true self and nature are not worthy enough for a plan to even be attached to.

Before the Most Honorable Elijah Muhammad, on page 129 introduces the reader to something called *'The Acceptance of the Divine Plan'*, He first teaches us Allah is God, Who the Original Man is and then He teaches us Islam. He gives us The True Knowledge of the Bible and the Holy Qur'an and explains The Making of the Devil. After we have learned this critical information, we then have the proper psychological orientation of the mind to develop and organize a plan that we might be able to make unlimited progress. Everything in the Scripture has a plan! No one just haphazardly thinks about a thing and then wishes for it, hopes for it and prays for it, and then sits on their hands and waits for it to happen. There is no mystery god!

When we look at the Hadith of Prophet Muhammad (PBUH), we learn that he was presented with a case for comparison of two kinds of believers. One man stayed in the Mosque, praying and as a result he became a very righteous individual. The other man was not as righteous, pure, or holy as this man was; however, he was greater at the propagation of the faith. Meaning, he was more productive for the community at large. When Prophet Muhammad (PBUH) was asked 'who is the greatest among the two', he is reported to have stated, *"The one that works the most."* Why? Because faith without works is dead.

Again, one man became individually righteous, but he failed to have an **impact** on others. Why, because the man that remained in the temple, praying and studying; yes, he became pure, but he did not have to plan anything because he was not working. Prophet Muhammad (PBUH) went on to say, *"This man that does all of that is weaker than the other because he has to wait for somebody else to come and feed him, but the other one goes out and finds a way to feed himself."*

Allah (God) Has A Plan

When we read the Holy Qur'an, we find Allah (God), Satan, the Jews, Pharaoh and disbelievers all have something in common. All of them have aims and goals meaning they did not sit around and wish or hope for something to happen. They planned to achieve what they desired. We read in Holy Qur'an 3:54 *"And (the Jews) planned and Allah (also) planned. And Allah is the best of planners."* This verse alone should help us all understand that a plan is so significant that The God, Himself, would make one. So, shouldn't we make one as well?

Satan tells God in the Bible, *"Surely, I shall lie in wait for them in thy straight path, and I shall make them all, deviate."* What Satan has done is given us the anatomy of the play that he is calling. The goal that Satan has set for himself is to produce deviation. God responds to Satan and tells him, *"You shall get all of them, except for my purified ones."* Why, because there is always an exception.

From the Holy Qur'an surah or chapter 103 we learn, *"By the time, surely man is in loss."* We must recognize that loss is taking place, in fact great loss right now, except for those *"who believe and do good and exhort one another to truth and exhort one another to patience."* Therefore, for most people in the world loss will happen but there is an exception. In this verse, those who believe and do good and exhort one another the truth and patience escape loss. In the previous verse Allah (God) says you will get all of them, except for my purified ones. The Holy Qur'an tells us that trials purify. Here is more mathematics! If trials, purify and purification keeps you from the reach of Satan, when trials come in our life, we should not say "why me?" We should say with excitement. "Try me!" Because it is successfully going through trials that purify us and purification makes us immune to Satan's plan. Jesus said be in the world, but not of the world. We can overcome the gravitational pull of this world.

The Most Honorable Elijah Muhammad refereed to this world, as a 6000-year vacuum. A vacuum can suck up small lightweight objects. So, the heavier we become in wisdom and deeds, we become an object that the suction of Satan is not powerful enough to pull into his hell.

How do we escape the gravitational pull of the world that is going down? We start exhorting more people to truth, exhorting more people to patience and doing more good, then as we believe, do good, exhort others to truth and have patience with self and others, we can step back and watch a world go down, while we come up. Remember, everyone did not go broke during the Great Depression or any of the subsequent recessions. In the book of Malachi, the last days are called the great, and the dreadful day of the Lord. Two opposite extremes existing in the same place at the same time. This could only be so if two different people are experiencing two different realities.

The last days are great for some (the purified ones, those who believe and do good, those who exhort one another the truth and exhort, one another to patience) and dreadful, for others (the wicked and the weak). Through study and application of Allah's Playbook, we can become the exception. While the week and the wicked are going broke, the righteous are getting rich. While the weak and the wicked are going insane, the righteous are growing in knowledge, wisdom, and understanding. While the weak and the wicked are miserable, unhappy, and depressed, the righteous live in a state of pure happiness.

Understand, we do not believe in a mystery god, nor do we believe in a mystery Satan. Satan and the devil are not one and the same. The Devil is the physical manifestation that embodies Satan, but Satan is the maker of Devil. Anything grafted from original can be called Devil. Satan can be negative spiritual qualities that can exist, even in the original people. For example, if we take a lighter and light the lighter, we know that there is fire produced that we can visibly see and if we touch it, it is hot—manifested physical reality. You could say that the fire is like the devil. Above that fire that we can physically see and touch, there is a pocket of air that if we touch it, even though we cannot see it, it can still produce a burn, just as bad as what we can see. That pocket of air that can burn us represents Satan. Allah (God) warns us in the Holy Qur'an, ***"Beware of the devil and his, hosts."***

A Host

A disease, if it is confined in a laboratory, has no power to affect or infect people. The disease will not gain momentum until the disease is released from the lab and finds a host and then the disease, acting through the host, begins to spread the sickness that first infected the host to others. In the book of Job 1:7, the question is raised, when the sons of God came to present themselves, *"...The Lord said unto Satan, Whence comest thou? Then Satan answered the LORD, and said, From going to and fro in the earth, and from walking up and down in it."* The sons of God were **with** Satan and did not know it. Meaning, Satan had to look like them and sound like them—Satan found a host to come in the form of.

Satan was there **with** them. He was saying, *'As Salaam Alaikum'. 'Walaikum Salaam.' 'How are you doing today?' 'I'm blessed and highly favored.'* Satan was there. Satan had taken on an identity that matched the identity of the group he was walking with. His language, his dress, his music all that matched the group on the surface, but Satan had a different motive in his heart than the rest that were called the Children of God. Understand, that one of the hardest lessons for many to learn is that we cannot take everyone with us because everyone is not with us. In 1John 2:19 we are told, **"They went out from us, but they were not of us; for if they had been of us, they would no doubt have continued with us: but they went out, that they might be made manifest..."**

When we are first introduced to Satan in the Bible, he shows up as a ventriloquist. Scripture says that the serpent deceived eve. We read about a snake in the garden, communicating with Adam and Eve. Snakes don't talk. Snakes do not have vocal cords. So, who is talking?

Satan is a ventriloquist in this context. Unfortunately, most of our entertainers are like puppets, also known as 'dummies' sitting on the lap of Satan himself. Our artists mouths are moving, but because Satan has his hand up their back in their pocket, his mind is coming through their mouth. This also happens right inside the ranks of our movements, and our mosques. We must remember that a circle cannot be destroyed from the outside in, it has to be imploded from the inside out. When we become a part of a group, we are in a circle of brotherhood, or a circle of sisterhood. Satan must work from within. Beware of the devil and his hosts.

The hypocrite is the devil's double. Those who are the withholders of their hand, and the lagers behind as the Holy Qur'an calls them, are Satan's spiritual counterparts inside the ranks. They say peace be unto you at 11 o'clock and 1:30pm they are gossiping and backbiting. They say, 'All Praise is due to Allah' at 12 and at 2pm they encourage a person to be immoral. They will say to us, 'It's Nation time,' at 3:15, but at 4 o'clock, start talking about how we got to try to look out for self. This is the way the enemy works. Robert Green in the book the **33 Strategies of War** explains, the old method of warfare is gone. The time of swords and spears of tanks and guns is done. The new form of war is not from the outside in, but it's from the inside out by the group or nations. From the people among them who engage in indifference and neglect. In other words, get those who are part of the Nation of Islam or any positive movement to disagree with leadership and good ideas. Get those who are in the Nation of Islam or any positive movement to begin to neglect doing their part, and you will not have to fire a shot, the Devil's Doubles will destroy them from within.

The last two chapters of the Holy Qur'an reveal part of how Satan's playbook is subtly instituted. In chapter 113 of the Holy Qur'an, it mentions the casting of an evil suggestion in firm resolutions. In chapter 114, it speaks of the evil of the whispering of the sinking devil. "Suggestions" "whisperings" not yelling, or issuing commands, He makes the firm resolution (good thing) and uses it as a package for his evil suggestion.

This enemy knows that everyone needs guidance. The first and greatest gift that Allah (God) ever gave us was the gift of life itself. The second most needed gift, after life comes into existence, is guidance. Every human being needs guidance because we are born into a world complete yet incomplete. We have the physical capacity to evolve and grow a body, we have fingers, toes, legs, hands, everything we need physically. What we lack though, is the immediate psychological and spiritual level of development necessary to allow us to properly use what we have, from the moment of birth. Complete physically, but incomplete spiritually and mentally.

Allah (God) Introduces Himself in the Holy Qur'an, *"I, Allah, am the Best Knower."* He did not say *I Allah, am a better knower.* That would leave room for us to think, something or someone could be the best. He eliminates the need for any deduction or reasoning on our part to compare Him, and what He teaches with anyone and what they teach. When we buy a car, it comes with an owner's manual. The owner's manual is guidance from the one who made this automobile, explaining how to get the best use of the automobile. We don't use the owner's manual from another brand of automobile. We know that if Honda made it, they are the ones qualified to tell us how to get the best use of it. Well, who manufactured you and me? Allah (God) says in the Holy Qur'an that I formed you in your mother's womb. And in the book of Jeremiah (Bible), God says *"I knew you before you were in your mothers womb and I formed you in your mother's womb.* Who then, is best to give us our "owner's manual?" Allah God's owner's manual, God's Playbook is found in the Bible, the Holy Qur'an, and the teachings of the Most Honorable Elijah Muhammad.

Fair-Seeming

Satan and Allah (God) are having a conversation in the Holy Quran 7:14, and within the conversation, Satan makes a request, *"Respite me until the day when they are raised."* The word respite is defined as to delay, my doom or my judgment. Allah (God) responds to Satan and says, **"Surely, thou shalt be of the respite ones."** Notice Satan did not ask for his doom to be delayed until August 1 of the year 2025. No time was issued. Satan asked can my judgment be delayed until the day when they are raised. Then if Satan's doom is delayed until the original man and the original woman are raised, we should know that Satan is going to do all in his power to keep (prevent) us from being raised. For when we are raised, his doom is sealed.

What produces the constant assault on The Honorable Minister Louis Farrakhan from our enemy? The origin of which can be found in the Counter Intelligence Program of J. Edger Hoover, with his primary pillar being, "preventing the rise of a black Messiah, who could unify any electrify..." After Allah respites Satan, Satan begins to boast, arrogantly and exposes his whole playbook. Though we were not present during the meeting when Satan was speaking to Allah (God), we have the minutes from the meeting. When a team is playing their opposition, but they are using the opposing team's whole playbook, shouldn't they win? We have no excuse to not win on this spiritual battlefield against Satan and his Minions. We have his whole playbook! Satan tells us that he is going to come in the straight path. Well, what is the straight path?

There are three primary areas which define the straight path, nature, religion and guidance. Satan is going to come clothed as an expert to offer guidance and to fill the psychological library with reference materials that is from a half-knower. He will come to corrupt nature and religion. Why in these three specific areas? Because his expressed goal is to cause as many as he can to deviate. He says, *"I shall make them all to remain disappointed, and you won't find most of them thankful."* Now, the agenda is very clear, the Satanic influence is coming in nature, to influence people to be disappointed, cause them to deviate and to be ungrateful.

To deviate means to turn aside as from a right way or course; to depart; as from a procedure, course of action, or acceptable norm; to digress as from a line of thought, of reasoning. To disappoint means to fail to fulfill expectations or the wishes of. To defeat the fulfillment of hopes, plans, etc... to thwart or to frustrate. Another aspect of Satan's plan found in his playbook is detailed in Holy Qur'an 4:119-excite in them vain desires and in 15:39, *make evil fair seeming.*

We must make sure we do not mismanage the emotions attached to these plays in Satan's Playbook:

1. Make them ungrateful

2. Cause them to remain disappointed

3. Make evil fair seeming

4. Excite in them vain desires

5. Make them all deviate

Divine Formula

The Honorable Minister Louis Farrakhan teaches that the God 'within' is not a spiritual person inside the body. *The God within are spiritual principles that live inside the mind.* In the **Self-Improvement Study Guide** entitled **The Will of God**, the Honorable Minister Louis Farrakhan states, *"The will is the real power of Allah (God) in man. However, the will must be buttressed or supported by faith and by knowledge. There is an emotional force that gives direction to the will, and that emotional force, which is the creative force upon which the entire universe is constructed, is love. It is out of this awesome power of love, that the will springs up. It (the will) springs up out of this emotion and is directed and guided by this emotion."*

When we unpack, the variables of this revolutionary statement made by the Honorable Minister Louis Farrakhan, We can see that Allah (God) within is made up of four distinct ingredients **will power, faith, knowledge** and **love**. The more willpower, faith, knowledge, and love that a person emanates from their being, the more of God is in the person.

From Holy Qur'an 53:39, we learn that man can have nothing, but what he strives for. Strive absolutely requires will power. the Honorable Minister Louis Farrakhan has stated, *"weak, willed persons, or persons,(is a person in whom the) the force of God is not strong. In fact, God 's spirit is as strong in the person as their will."* Will power is mental muscle. Will power is what gives your muscle strength that they it does not possess on its own. Wheel power allows the physical muscles to tap into a spiritual power from the mind that allows the physical muscle to do more than even what it is conditioned to do. When we use **will power, faith, knowledge,** and **love** (the God

Within) properly, we, too, can say, be and it is. The Honorable Minister Louis Farrakhan, in the same study guide on the Will of God, says, *That when Allah says Be! This is an expression of His will, but it is more than just an expression of His will, for when He says Be! He arranges forces, resources, angels, and people, according to a plan to bring about the fruition of His will. Allah's will never fails.*

This divine formula is how the God brings things into existence, and this divine formula is what we have to follow. If we are going to be a god that can do the same. In this world, they suggest to man that you either work hard or you work, smart. The truth is if we are following this divine formula, it shows that we have to work righteously, smart, and hard.

Prayerize, Visualize, and then Actualize! Just as in the Mosque and the Church, all things are opened in prayer, so should all our plans be opened in prayer because prayer strengthens faith. When we are talking the word of God, we are strengthening our faith. When we are quoting passages from the Bible and Holy Qur'an, we are strengthening our faith. When we go deeper through the study of the quotes of the Bible and the Holy Qur'an, using science and nature, history and mathematics become supporting knowledge helping to validate what the faith has rendered. Faith is increased by the word of God being expressed. Knowledge is increased by the supporting evidence given to man to justify what we believe in.

This is the fundamental difference between Faith and Blind Faith. Blind Faith has no basis in knowledge. However, real faith is supported by logic, reasoning, deduction, analyzation, and facts. Evidence converts beliefs into convictions, and convictions, gives your mind permission to throw your whole self at an endeavor. When we throw our whole self at an endeavor, we increase the probability of success. When we throw our whole self, meaning we gave our all, or at the scripture we stated earlier, did it with all of our might, There is something about knowing that you left it all on the field that the result becomes secondary to the mental satisfaction of knowing you did the best you could do. Sometimes our best is not good enough to achieve the objective at the time we thought we should, but where there is life there is hope. So, if we are blessed with an opportunity to reflect and come back at the task, and make our best, better, the probability of success is increased, even more.

Successful people are not easily distracted. The orientation of their mind is focused on their goals. They do not spend all day playing video games. Understand, it is not a coincidence that it is called the world wide web, a web is a trap laid by a spider. The job of a spider, after the prey gets caught in the web, is to wait patiently for the prey, to get tired of fighting to free itself from the web. Once the prey is so exhausted from trying to free itself the spider crawls along the web and then sticks a needle into the brain of the prey. This needle-like object injects a poisonous enzyme into the prey. The enzyme works to break down the interior body of the prey into liquid, then the spider sucks all the insides out of its prey, leaving only the preys outside intact. The insect caught in the web looks like it is OK in this web. So other insects flying by think it's safe to land, but when they do, if they do not get out of the web within three seconds, they are stuck. So, it is with the world wide web. Social media is full of prey that looks good on the outside, but the insides have been sucked completely out. A body with no soul. Talent with no integrity. The Holy Qur'an describes People who have been flipped as pieces of wood clad in garment. Like wood has no spirit no soul no intellect so it is with us the more time we spend looking down at our phones or tablets. Behavioral scientists have proved that psychology affects physiology. This is where the study of body language came from. When a person is curious, they lean in and listen. When a person is disinterested, they slumped and look away etc. Well, for every action, there is in nature an equal and opposite reaction.

So, the act of asking psychologically affects physiology, and physiology can affect psychology as well. I a picture once that was really shameful. It was a picture of people in a rush walking through traffic in New York City. It was a shame. On both sides of the street hundreds of people were walking down the street but almost all of them were looking down at their phone. If physiology can affect psychology, then, when we constantly look down physically it is only a matter of time before we begin to look down mentally. We are dealing with the mathematics of the mind. Nicholas Kardares, in his book, "**Digital Heroine**," showed by using functional magnetic resonance imaging (fMRI), that excessive screen time had the same neurological effects on the brain as drugs. Excessive screen time. Excessive screen time--social media, etc. The insect had three seconds to get out of the web before he became the prey. Now admittedly, I am not sure exactly what three seconds would look like for us in the web of social media; however, suffice it to say it should be a small portion of the time that we engage social media throughout our day. In order to prevent our mental and spiritual insides from being sucked out.

The Honorable Minister Louis Farrakhan explained that *"Social media is neutral."* When our car breaks down what do we put it in? We put it in neutral, because it can then go in any direction with less resistance, forward or backward. Then if social media is neutral, then social media can propel us forward or it can send us backward and degenerate us. The Honorable Minister Louis Farrakhan said, ***"Master Fard Muhammad gave us the Supreme Wisdom and the white man gave us Facebook. Use it to promote Supreme Wisdom*** *and then it won't be neutral going backwards into degradation. It would be neutral propelling us forward into being a god."*

We must self-regulate and monitor ourselves, our thoughts, at all times. **We should never spend more time on Facebook than we do in our 'Faith book'!** We can use technology as a means for us to make progress faster; however, we cannot allow our time and thoughts to be controlled by this technology. Use it as a tool, a weapon and an instrument to speed up time so that the lion can get out of this 2,000 by 3,000-mile cage called the wilderness of North America, faster.

FYI: The Restrictive Laws still live in cyberspace. Allah (God) does not want to see how good we are when there is no evil around. The real question and challenge is, can we be *in* the world and not *of* the world. Can we be in hell and elevate our consciousness so much that truly the real Kingdom of God is within? When we have so much love for God and so much character, that no matter where we are and who we are around, we are never persuaded by them to lower our moral standards. This is what real righteousness looks like. Real righteousness is when you can stand and truthfully say 'I did a lot in the known world and went many places and I was tempted by many things and even under temptation, I still kept my principles.' WE have to remember that we are 'God's Social Media!' The God is not after likes. He's after lives, and He wants to use us to get them!

Understanding and Working With the Laws

Inside of the universe, there exists a multi-layered matrix of laws in a duality. There are laws that govern the 'do' and 'do not' of existence itself. Some laws that exist are 'do not' centered and others are 'do' centered. Anytime we hear the mention of law we automatically assume that it is talking about what not to do. Just like we have laws to stop negative action, there are also laws that activate positive action. There is a law of Cause and Effect; there are Laws of Success. There is a Law of Gravity, a Law of Buoyancy, a Law of Reciprocity, a Law of Use and the much talked about Law of Attraction to name only a few. These laws are not 'do not' laws, these are do laws. These are laws that must be executed because they require action and activity to be *activated*. We have to be careful not to be under the illusion that we are good or great, because we did not do anything bad. Goodness and greatness do not come from just not doing wrong. It also requires a certain amount of doing of right. In the Holy Qur'an, there is not a verse that says successful, indeed are those who believe and do not do any wrong, but several times you *read successful are those who believe and do good.* Success is not just attached to one that believes. We must believe and execute the 'do' laws if we really want to be successful.

In Holy Qur'an 9:72, Allah (God) tells us what the real grand achievement is, ***"And the greatest of all is Allah's goodly pleasure. That is the grand achievement.*** "Allah (God) does not leave it up to us, to guess what the grand achievement is, because had we guessed, we might have taken on the definition of achievement or success that this world has to offer. In the world we live in today, success is not even spelled with an 's'. In this world, they have replaced all the 's' with a dollar sign ($). So, success in this world is money and power. It is fame or status in life.

When time permits, write out a list of all the names of people you personally consider to be successful. After the list is complete, review it and what you will realize is that everyone we define, in our minds as successful, has either money, fame, power or status. Truthfully, this is not 100% wrong to have or possess, because Master Fard Muhammad instructs us to, *"Sit yourself in heaven at once."* The difference is that He explicitly described what heaven actually is for us. Master Fard Muhammad explained that ***Heaven*** is *"Luxury Money, Good homes and friendship in all walks of life."* So, in the precise mathematical equation we have fame, status, power and money. What makes the success that Master Fard Muhammad is describing so different is that this success does not start from the outside in. It starts from the *inside out* with obedience to Allah (God's) will that produces freedom, justice, equality, harmony, balance, peace and contentment of mind within the being. To the degree that we submit to his word, and do his work, is to the degree that we reap the spiritual and physical fruits He promised. When a person has peace, contentment of mind, harmony, balance, freedom, justice, and equality, they will begin to manifest that spirit. The Most Honorable Elijah Muhammad said the outside reflects the inside. The heaven within is then reflected on the outside, in physical health and mental quickness.

Anyone who thinks they have friends because they have money, the sad reality is that you do not have real friends. When the money's gone, we find out who our real friends are. When we see very famous people with a large entourage, that they call their friends, they are not even friends to them. They are not in a relationship with the person. They are not really connected to the person they are connected to what the person has (material possessions and fame). But the minute the money dries up, the minute their ability to fulfill a need is gone, where is the so-called friend? They are gone because they never were real friends, they were just an associate and a blood sucker. Real friends are not connected to a person based on the amount of money in a person's pocket. Friends are connected because of the principles that you order and live your life by, and the agreeable personality you possess. The hard truth is that even if you had no money, you would still have your principles and your personality and if they could be with you in those moments, they are a true friend.

Divine Priority

The Most Honorable Elijah Muhammad teaches that the brain of man is infinite. To be infinite, means there is no stopping point, no break point, to which the brain or mind can be stretched or can achieve. We live in a universe that is 76 quintillion miles in diameter, giving it a circumference of 238 quintillion 740 quadrillion, 120 trillion miles in circumference. The Honorable Elijah Muhammad teaches that, the universe is a copy of the original God, who was a man, not vice versa. This means if the universe matches the mind, when the mind is expanded, the universe has to follow. So, if the brain of man reaches to new heights of wisdom, then the physical universe in which we live, must also expand to a whole new dimension unknown to the present world, this present reality. Infinite.

Since the brain of man is infinite, and the universe *reflects* the brain, then we do not move when the stars say so, the stars move when we say so. We are the gods; not of some finite location, we are the god of the Universe. Which means we possess sole control and authority over every molecule, atom, quark and quantum that exists in the material world, by the power of our mind!

Allah (God) in Holy Qur'an 71:13 asks, *"What is the matter with you that you hope not for greatness from your Lord?"* In other words, why are we content with the little power we execute? Why is it okay to just be an *average* person. Why do we not desire optimal health? We were born to achieve the grand achievement! The grand achievement is not merely believer, follower, companion, disciple, or apostle. Allah (God) desires to make each of us into a god, a perfect reflection of Him. When we look at Holy Qur'an 20:2 Allah (God) says, *"We did not reveal the Qur'an to you that you would be unsuccessful."* Holy Qur'an 23:1 says, *"You can tell the believers, they are the successful ones."* Understand, that Allah (God) wants us to be successful to proser and live in peace. No where does it say that God wants us to be poor, naked raggedy, hungry and out of doors homeless. NO WHERE. We must get rid of the idea that there is a deity whose will it is that you should be poor, or whose purposes may be served by keeping you in poverty.

John 10:10 says, *"I came that you may have life and have it more, abundantly"* the question is what is life? Life represents energy. Life represents joy. Life represents happiness. So, if Allah (God) came that we might have life and have life more abundantly, then this is the goal of Allah (God) concerning us. God has established Divine Priority, and the top priority is laid before us in 3 John 1:2, *"Above all things, I wish that you would prosper. And be in good health, even as thy soul prospereth."* There are three clear and distinct categories that God wants us to see achievement in presented here. He wants us to have economic progress, to have good health and He wants our soul; in fact, He said, *"Even as thy soul prospereth."* Even means on the same level as. So, we cannot work more on money and on muscle than we do on morals. Even as the soul prospereth, our primary energy then must be invested in the cultivation of the god within—*self-improvement.*

When we strive hard to build the god within up, by cultivating Christ Consciousness, then we have the moral character needed to support having large sums of money. If we go to the gym all the time and eat perfectly, but we do not have the character necessary to support health and money, we fall into the sins of the flesh without thinking about them. We become an adulterer or a fornicator more easily because we have no moral compass to guide us while we navigate having these great sums of money and the power it brings with it. A sister who used to be modest will no longer cover herself because she is on social media and wants the attention that showing her body will bring her—no moral standards.

When we have Christ Consciousness, we do not cultivate the body, or seek optimal health for vanity so we can show off our form, male or female. We get in shape to be a better weapon and tool in the hand of God for building the Kingdom of God. When we have money and we have our character intact and our soul has been fed, we do not floss the money by acquiring things that appease the vanity of our senses. We use the abundance of financial resources that God has provided us with to make investments that evolve to create avenues for others to be successful and to learn the principles of success.

The Honorable Minister Louis Farrakhan teaches, *"money will come with true service, but when money is the focal point, it robs you of the real spirit that God wants you to have that will make you successful in all you do."* The Honorable Minister Louis Farrakhan went on to say, *"don't be afraid to make each other rich. The rich man should be ashamed of getting rich off of his people, and then do nothing for the community that made him rich."*

The Law of Attraction is a key law co-existing with The Law of Cause and Effect. The Law of Cause and Effect really is The Law of Attraction when understood properly. The Law of Attraction is working, all the time, whether we believe, understand, or accept it. It is a law that does not consider what a person thinks. It operates in the universe. The Bible, bears witness to this fact in Proverbs 10:24, *"What evil people dread most will happen to them, but good people will get what they want the most."* The Law of Attraction works for the good and the evil. It is still The Law of Attraction working, it is just that the good one receives the positive and the evil one receives the negative.

In Proverbs 21:2 we read, *"For you have given King David his heart's desire. You did not refuse his request. You have blessed him greatly."* Well, if it is his heart's desire, there is no record in Proverbs of David praying and asking for anything. Therefore, this means that the heart's desire was the request. David did not even have to put it in word form, and it is here that we discover where we are struggling with the math the most. We fail to realize that what we are thinking about all the time, is actually a prayer that we are requesting from Allah (God), whether we know it or not.

Thought is a Seed

When what we think constantly of and on is the negative, what we are doing is asking Allah (God) to grant our request for the negative. This negative thought pattern (cycle of thinking) represents the real desires of our heart. *'Oh, Allah please surround me with negative people, negative circumstances. Please give me negative situations and events that can help me produce the greatest catastrophe You can muster up.'* Whatsoever a man soweth, the same shall he reap. Whatever a person believeth in or asketh and believeth, they shall receive. Our problem is that we have never connected asking or sowing to thinking. ***Thought is a seed.***

When someone says a person dropped a seed on them, what does this mean? No one places inside of a man or woman's ear a physical seed. What the seed represents is a certain word, containing a particular electrical charge that went into the mind and produced the thought in the person's head. Therefore, if dropping a seed is another way of saying, forming a thought in someone's head with a word, then *thinking is sowing.* Thinking is requesting. The Law of Attraction then means what we think we can bring into existence. **Your life is your mind turned inside out!**

The Law of Attraction can be summarized, *"as a man or woman thinketh in their heart, so is he or she."* What the world presents as the Law of Attraction is an idea devoid of the essential parts which then creates a false, yet profitable market, where it is necessary to buy books and attend seminars to learn more. They have deceived people into thinking that all one must do is sit around and think about whatever they want to be, do, or have. This gives the false idea and hope that if they sit still and think about things hard enough, these thoughts will form ideas and my ideas will begin to clothe me with everything I want to be, do, and have. This is the core of mystery god belief, if we do nothing, good will just magically appear out of the sky. However, **a do-nothing mentality will produce a have nothing in reality.**

All of this is false teachings. Faith without work is dead. Prophet Muhammad (PBUH) said, *"Mere belief counts for nothing except it is carried into practice."* From the world of psychology, we learn that affirmation, without discipline, is the beginning of disillusionment. But affirmations with discipline attached to them, is the beginning of the working of miracles. Dr. Maya Angelou said it best, *"Nothing will work unless you do."*

The Law of Attraction must lead to The Law of Action. And when we practice The Law of Attraction, thinking right, living right, being moral, being honorable, being motivated purely, then we begin to turn ourselves into living magnets. When we become a living magnet, we begin to attract to us people, circumstances, events and situations that match the nature of our dominant thought, our dominant vibrational level. If we are willing to take advantage of the opportunity and act on what we have attracted, then we will be successful. In the end, the absolute truth is as the Holy Qur'an 13:11 reminds us, *"Surely Allah changes not the condition of a people, until they change their own condition."* In the Nooridin translation of the Holy Qur'an this same verse reads, *"Allah (God) will not change the condition of a people until they change their **thoughts** and their **ways** (actions)."* The law of attraction and the law of Action working in concert with one another.

The Battlefield of the Mind

When we study the animal kingdom, we find not only a hierarchical system of organization we also find, just as in human life, there exist things that eat death itself. In the animal kingdom, the only creatures that actively seek out dead things are buzzards, the scavengers of the land. The things in nature that feed on the dead are the most abject among the animal kingdom itself. They are by characteristic, low down, dirty and lazy. The buzzard, like ravens, shrimp, catfish and lobster, does not hunt for food like all other living animals. These creatures just sit around at the bottom of existence itself and feed off the death and decay of others.

We are what we eat, on all levels. A thought directs and even trains the mind, so a steady diet of death in the form of food, music, movies etc., trains the mind to think like death. If everything that is in existence, that lives from the dead, is itself a low-life animal that is lazy (lacking in self-determination), then the more we are attached to what is death, the more like a buzzard rat, catfish, scavenger we become. We become a lazy, nonproductive, dependent person; waiting on some living hunter, to kill something so that we can eat the waste.

There is no heaven that is without work. This is spookism. What is spookism? It is an extreme or excessive emotional attachment to a non-existent nothing! In order to have a real heaven, somebody must swing a hammer, work and till the ground, plant the seeds and reap the harvest. Then others must package, distribute, and sell the fruits of the labor. *Heaven is a working environment*. The difference is that it is a happy working environment. With clean air and good people.

The Honorable Minister Louis Farrakhan said, *"The only way we can change as a people is if we change the way we think."* He went on to say, *"Thought is the power that created the Universe and all therein."* The Bible (John 1:1) puts it this way, *'In the beginning was the word. The word was God, the word was with God, the world became flesh.'* A word starts off as a thought. And then thought marries sound and produces a word. A word has a mother and a father called thought and sound.

Again, as we learned in earlier chapters, The Honorable Elijah Muhammad taught that an atom could successfully be cracked into 10 million parts. The Caucasian scientist of this world never believed that an atom could be cracked at all, let alone into 10 million parts. In their thought process, the atom was the smallest particle of matter. In April 1932, they cracked an atom. They cracked it once and found in it a quark, a particle smaller than an atom yet containing all the ingredients of the atom. Then they cracked the quark and found what today is known as the quantum. A quantum is in fact a thought. The Honorable Elijah Muhammad said if we crack open an atom, we can see everything in the Universe *inside* the atom. We just have to have a device more powerful than a microscope to see it. A microscope can only see the physical. So, there must be a way to see the spiritual because thought is spiritual. All things are composed, on the cellular level of atoms and inside the center of an atom, the idea of the whole Universe is present. Inside of every single atom of life is the Universe itself.

Returning to John 1:1, what we now understand is that in the beginning was a thought. A thought traveling at 24 billion miles per second on average, which is connected to something traveling at 1,120 feet per second is called sound. When thought and sound come together, they can produce something called word. Words, then become actions. Actions become habits. And habits form character and character, dictates destiny or future. In other words, becomes flesh, and dwells among men. The Sun is a thought. The moon, the stars, the birds, the bees, this is all a manifestation of thought!

Thought, travels at the speed of 24 billion miles per second. If we slow it down to 186,000 miles per second, then thought becomes light. Slow it down further to 1,120 feet per second, then it manifests as sound. Slow it down to 1,037 1/3 miles per hour and we have the Earth, we have Pluto, we have Mercury, we have grass, we have trees, we have rocks. All that we are seeing is the manifestation of thought functioning at varying vibratory rates. This is why Allah (God) is the only Reality. Allah (God) is the only reality because everything comes from Him. The Honorable Minister Louis Farrakhan stated during a lecture entitled *Let Us Make Man* delivered in Chicago, Illinois, *"Thought is so powerful that even though it is immaterial, it is the essence of everything you see."*

Proverbs 23:7 says, *"As a man thinketh in his heart,"* The heart being referred to here is not the one that pumps blood, it is in fact referring to the core of the mind. Solomon is using the heart as an analogy, so that we can study deeper into a principle, a law. The heart found in our physical chest generates (moves) the blood created by the bone marrow and pumps the blood through 60,000 miles of veins and arteries. As it circulates the blood it also carries within it commands data and nutrients to all parts of the body to help us function properly. The heart is the source that pumps physical life. Yet, if the heart works on someone in the hospital but their brain does not, that person is considered dead. When the brain works, but the heart has stopped, the doctors can use a defibrillator and shock the heart back into sinus rhythm. Making it possible for someone to come out of the condition they are in. This should tell us without a doubt that the spiritual is more important than the physical.

Have you ever gotten sleep from sitting still? This happens because a high level of inactivity becomes fatigue. What causes us to become so physically tired if we have not exerted significant amounts of energy? We become tired because we are constantly wrestling with our thoughts. We are wrestling with problems, excuses, with our own weakness, and even though we may sit still we get tired because of a mind war. This is why we are cautioned in the Bible to, *'set your minds and keep them set on what is above, the higher things, not on the things that are on the earth.'* Philippians4:8 states, *Finally, brethren, whatsoever things are true, whatsoever things are honest, whatsoever things are just, whatsoever things are pure, whatsoever things are lovely, whatsoever things are of good report; if there be any virtue, and if there be any praise, think on these things.* It is universally accepted in psychology that negative thoughts consume more mental emotional energy than positive thoughts. When we dwell on negative thoughts, it can lead to increased stress, anxiety, and even physical tension in the body, which in turn drains energy.

There is an ancient Navajo parable, where a grandfather is advising his grandson. He tells his grandson, *"Grandson, inside of me lives two wolves. One wolf is a good wolf that loves and is compassionate and it lives truly. While the other wolf is dishonest and corrupt and lives badly. Everyday there's a fight going on inside of me between these two wolves."* The grandson asks, *"Well grandfather, which one wins?"* The grandfather responds, *"Whichever one I feed the most."*

Unlimited Power

Jesus is, according to both the Bible and Holy Qur'an, the supreme example of what a man or woman can become. Paul, in Philippians 2:5, when speaking of Jesus says, *"Let this mind be in you, the same mind that was in Christ Jesus."* In Proverbs 23:7 we read, *"As a man thinketh in his heart, so is he."* If the followers of Jesus are being invited to have the same mind that Jesus had, and Jesus had the mind of God, then if we adopt the mind of Jesus, which is the mind of God, knowing and accepting that as a man and woman thinketh in their heart so are they, then we become a god!

We read in Luke 17:21 Jesus says, *"The Kingdom of God (Heaven) is within you."* The kingdom is the place where the king lives. Meaning, that God lives within us. God lives, God rests, God abides, makes decisions, and exercises His authority, not from somewhere in outer space, but right inside of our own brains. From the Bible in 2 Timothy 1:7, *'For God did not create us in the spirit of timidity, but a spirit of power, of love and self-discipline.'* Some translations say in place of self-discipline. Sound mind, but without self-discipline, we will never have a sound mind. **Self-discipline is self-love!** The original spirit of unlimited power, given to us by God, to access it and to use it, we must exercise ever increasing levels of self-discipline which then nurtures the seed of what Allah (God) gave us. This seed, when fully mature is called unlimited power. Energy is constant. It just changes forms.

God created us in the spirit. Where does the spirit live? The spirit lives in our soul. Our soul lives in our heart. Again, our heart does not live in our chest cavity. When Jesus says, *"As a man thinketh in his heart,"* He is speaking to us about an *idea* that occupies the core of the mind. Spirit is in the soul, soul is in the heart, heart is in the mind, mind is in the brain. Brain is in the body. The power is not out there (external), the power is right inside of our minds (internal).

Allah (God), in Holy Qur'an 11:7, *"And He it is who created the heavens and the earth in six periods. And his thrown of power..."* His thrown of what? If the kingdom is where the king dwells and the place where the king exercises his authority and his decision making over his subjects, inside of the kingdom is a throne. A specific fixed position where the king sits to dwell and to make choices. If Allah (God) in the Holy Qur'an is saying that the throne of power is ever upon water, there is no big gold chair in the middle of the ocean with the Supreme Being sitting on it. Just as a land mass surrounded by water on the planet is called an island, the brain is an island.

The throne of Allah's (God's) power is ever upon water, then this must be the brain, for the brain sits on water. *'How do we know?'* When we read the entire verse, we learn: *"The throne of Allah's power is ever on water that He might manifest the good qualities in you."* Well, if God's out in the middle of the ocean, His position would be where He could manifest the good qualities in the fish, the dolphin, but not us. If His throne of powers is on water that He might manifest the good qualities *in* us, then God is posted up, dwelling, exercising authority, making decisions from our brain. Why? To show us the unlimited power that we all possess.

When the Muslim comes to prayer, we hear "Hayya 'alas-Salat. Hayya 'alas-Salat." Twice which translates into, *"Come to prayer."* Then we hear, *"Hayya 'alal-Falah,"* twice. *"Come to cultivation. Come to success."* What is cultivation? Cultivation is the feeding and the weeding of a seed that is already planted. The definition of cultivation, according to the dictionary, is to promote the growth and development of. When one cultivates a seed, the seed is already planted.

Allah (God) is telling us to come to prayer and come to cultivation. He is instructing us that the seed of God, His very essence, is already within us. This seed must be nurtured, sustained, and fed. It must become fruitful in order to multiply. It must be grown, matured, and developed so that it can bear fruit, repeatedly, over time—without limit or end. If we take a tree as an analogy for the man and woman, we can see that a tree begins with a round seed under the Earth. That round seed, under the Earth begins to develop a shoot. The shoot becomes a trunk. From that trunk comes branches. And from those branches comes fruit. When we hear the phrase, 'The fruits of someone's labor?' we now understand that the fruit we harvest is in direct proportion to our actions and strivings.

Let us think deeply about this, a round seed brought birth to a trunk that produced branches, that produced fruit. The seed is a metaphor for the right kind of thought, right kind of idea in the mind. So, like the branches extend out from a tree, so do our arms and legs. The branches produce fruit, and our hands produce the fruit of our labor. Then the throne of Allah's (God's) power, being ever upon water, means that He, God Himself, has planted inside of us the potential for unlimited power, unlimited progress.

The Arabic word Farmer is 'Fellaheen' coming from its root word Falah (Cultivation/Success). Telling us that success comes when we are good farmers of the seed of divine that is planted in us. A good farmer is vigilant, always making sure, that no foreign agent such as a weed grows unchecked ultimately causing the seed we planted not to develop as fully as it could develop. It is the job of the farmer to fertilize that seed, to keep the soil rich with minerals, to keep it in a position and state where it receives adequate sunlight and water. A wise farmer knows that if he is careful to provide for the seed, the seed will mature to its fullest extent. So, it is with you and I, God is a seed inside of us. To access and use this unlimited power, we must weed out the mind. Feed the mind good water, good light, good soil. (Spiritual knowledge, wisdom, understanding, and good physical food)

The Bible teaches that Jesus was exalted to the right hand of the Father. Jesus cultivated the seed of God within himself to such a degree that he could boldly say, without fear of being contradicted, *"I and my Father are One. When you see me, you see the Father."* Why? 'Because I have completely submitted to Him. I do not do what I want to do. I do what He wants me to do. I think like He thinks. I do what He said for me to do.' Jesus told the people, when they said of him, *"Thou good master."* He said, *"Why calleth thou me good? There's none good but the Father."* (Mark 10:8) Then He said, *"I of my own self can do nothing."* (John 5:30) Jesus recognized that everything was *Insh'allah.* Everything was *'if it be the will of Allah.'* Jesus, in John 16:13 states, *"Whatsoever I heareth, that shall I speak." "Whatsoever the Father commandeth me to do, that shall I do."* (John 14:31) In John 6:38 Jesus says, *"It's not my will that I do, but it is the will of the Father who hath sent me."* How is this all possible, because he gave himself entirely over to the cultivation of the seed of God within him.

Will Power

The Honorable Elijah Muhammad teaches that heaven and hell are not places, they are states of mind, states of being, and conditions of life. Every thought produces a word. Every word becomes an action. All actions, taken together, make your habits. Habits make your character. Character dictates how your future is composed. Where are you going to be in five years? Examine your thinking today; how we think, will produce a word like unto itself. That word will produce actions which mirror our thinking. Those actions will become habits, meaning we will be doing and acting from the thought pattern which most closely mirrors our daily thinking—positive or negative, good or bad.

In physics, the formula for power is work divided by time ($P=W/t$). Machines are designed to do work on an object; a person is also designed by Allah (God), not just to pray, think or read, but to work; to have an effect and an impact on the material world. The machine and the man, both have a power rating. A machine's power rating is called watts, or wattage, sometimes horsepower. *The human wattage rate is called willpower.* There are those among us who, like machines, are more powerful than others. Take note of the suffix, 'ful', powerful, full of power. Some have been born with a greater inherent endowment of power than others, though all people have the capacity to acquire unlimited power.

How are we able to determine whether something is more powerful in machines or even in humans? Some people can do the same amount of work in less time as another person. Then some people can do more work, in the same amount of time, as another person. We have all been a witness to this before. When one can do

NURI MUHAMMAD

the same task that took someone 30 minutes to complete in 15 minutes, we can conclude that they have more power. When two people are engaged in the same activity of production for 30 minutes, one produces 20 units and the other produces 50 units. The one that produced more in the same amount of time is more powerful.

Power is not something we just pray for, wish for and hope for. Unlimited power is something we were all born with. What is different is the rate and dedication to the cultivation of the power within to do more. We must be cultivated so that when we come to prayer, we are truly coming to cultivation for it is the cultivation of the mind and spirit that produces success.

It is dangerous to assume, using this world as the rod of comparison, that when we see one that is a failure and another that is a successful person, that their success or failure is solely based upon one knowing more than another person knows. This is not a constant fact. There are people who can pontificate, articulate, regurgitate, memorize, and recite the Holy Qur'an and the Bible from one cover to the next. But they cannot take care of their own son or daughter. Cannot put food on the table for their own self let alone a family. This is a person that knows more but is not more powerful than the one who works hard to be a provider.

The assumption that success and failure is totally hinged on knowledge is not true. It is primarily the use of knowledge upon which success and failure hinge. When people say, *'Knowledge is power,'* no it is not. Knowledge is power, only if the one that has it, uses it. If knowledge is not activated and put into service, it is of no significance. A person that has access to knowledge but will not activate it and use it is what the Holy Qur'an calls a jackass (donkey) carrying books. **It** is not enough to know what to do after we know what to do we must do what we know!

The Honorable Minister Louis Farrakhan teaches, *"The fire of hell is a mental scorching from the consequences of choices that we have or have not made."* A mental scorching. Frustrated, meaning the minds on fire. Stressed out. The National Library of Medicine recorded in March 2023 that procrastination is one of the top causes of stress. The mind is on fire--mental scorching. Why? Because we are putting off till tomorrow something that should have been done yesterday! In the Holy Qur'an, 18:23, we read," and *say not to anything I will do that tomorrow."* **Procrastination is Anti-God!** The consequences of not doing what we are supposed to do begins playing over and over in the mind as an endless loop. That is hell.

Jesus and Muhammad are the supreme examples of tapping into and the cultivation of unlimited power. They did this by first, recognizing and acknowledging that there is no God but Allah. After they recognized there was no God, but Allah and they submitted to that God, then they began to study to become intelligent, wise people. They studied so that they could work better, more intelligently in the identification and tackling of problems and challenges. Jesus said you shall know the truth, and the truth shall make you free. Jesus could state this because he lived free by his study and application of the Truth. Prophet Muhammad (PBUH) said, *"seek knowledge from the cradle to the grave."* In another Hadith (saying), Prophet Muhammad stated that *"man is on the path of God when he seeks knowledge until, he returns."* Jesus and Prophet Muhammad did not just pray and fast, they had a healthy respect for the acquisition and application of knowledge.

Supreme Discipline

There is a popular concept used today called, 'level up.' Of course, this term is not found in the dictionary. Level up is only a term, or idiom found in urban culture. In fact, it is a phrase that we as Black people borrowed from the video gaming world. In the world of video games, when a certain level of achievement occurs, when a player, for example, is rewarded with a large amount of digital currency or new powers. Or some features of the tools, already in possession of the player are unlocked, then the player is said to have 'leveled up. '

When one truly levels up, in real life, this means to consistently make moves with the intent in mind to become better. In life, there is no hack or cheat code. There is no trick that can be performed. In real life, there is no power pellet we can eat. Leveling comes from a campaign of discipline. Consistently doing what you should do, when you should do it, whether you feel like doing it or not.

There is no success. There is no moving beyond where we are without pushing ourselves. There is no leveling up without working past fatigue; without maintaining a course of action, long after the excitement has worn off. Nothing will work unless we do. Leveling up requires prayer, faith in Allah (God), faith in self without arrogance, a plan, and consistent action. To level up you cannot quit when you are tired. You quit when you are done!

One of the primary reasons upward motion in life is stopped is because a person thinks they have already arrived. When we think we have already arrived, this is arrogance. Arrogance, the Honorable

Minister Louis Farrakhan said, has a blinding quality to it. Arrogance disallows a person to see other people properly. While this is bad, what is worse is that arrogance disallows a person from truly seeing themselves. *Arrogance always destroys opportunity.*

Arrogance weakens productivity. Arrogant people do not like getting their hands dirty. *'That's beneath me'* is the mindset and anyone that is aspiring to leadership, know this, **if service is beneath you, then leadership is beyond you.** Leadership is about service, not about self. To level up we have to be humble *and* hungry!

If we are without, it is because we have not taken the steps necessary to increase our capacity to obtain and maintain what we desire. Increasing our knowledge is critical to leveling up. What we do not have is a direct result of what we do not know. Another reason we do not have what we want to have is because we are operating on the same level—we are comfortable and we are unwilling to become uncomfortable. Where there is no disciple, there is no love. The Honorable Minister Louis Farrakhan has stated, ***"We will not become a strong people unless we become a disciplined people."*** He teaches that, ***"To be disciplined means to have your life ordered by principles."*** **We have in one of our writings, Being disciplined does not mean that I'm being punished, but I'm learning to place the goal of my unit or team above my own personal desires. And in so doing, I am learning Supreme Discipline, the kind that saves lives and wins battles.** With supreme discipline, we can defeat the battle we have without bowing to our lower desires. With Supreme Discipline, we can defeat procrastination, laziness, excuse making, weakness, fault finding, finger pointing, blame gaming. With Supreme Discipline, we take 100% authority over ourselves, and we become self-motivated: a self-starter.

Like Big Momma used to say, and truth be told, she said it so much we grew up thinking it was an actual Bible verse: *'God helps those who help themselves.'* The Holy Qur'an clarifies it all for us in Surah 13:11, *"Allah changes not the condition of a people until that people change their own condition."* In the Noorudin translation of the Holy Qur'an we read the same verse this way, *"Until the people change their thoughts and ways."* The formula the Holy Qur'an and the Bible gives for leveling up is the same, no matter which one we reference: to be transformed we must renew our mind (thinking) and by renewing our mind, we produced renewed actions.

Self-disciplined

Fundamentally, there are two types of discipline. One is *self-discipline* and the other is *supplementary discipline.* Supplementary discipline is discipline from the *outside in.* Self-discipline is control and self-governing according to principles from the *inside out.* Supplementary discipline is not for a fully developed person. A fully developed person does not need someone to give them an order because they are already in order. If a person is already in order, no one has to put them back in order. Self-motivated people do not need someone to tell them what to do, they are already doing it. So, supplementary discipline is the process by which we learn how we should operate by ourselves. We learn this by operating around someone or some system greater than ourselves, and because we are operating with someone or some system greater than ourselves, we will have discipline imposed from the outside in, temporarily.

The aim is and should always be, to graduate from a disciple to an apostle. As we can see, the words disciple and discipline share the same phonetic and etymological word base. A disciple is one who is disciplined from the outside in while an apostle is one who is disciplined from the inside out. While Jesus was with the twelve, they were called his disciples. When Jesus was gone, they graduated from disciples into apostles because they did not have supplementary discipline being imposed from the outside in any longer. They evolved in their faith and developed self-discipline from the inside out.

Self-discipline is when a man or a woman has an iron will; mental strength; inner strength and drive. Self-discipline means they have principles in their mind, and they do not need a person outside of self to remind them; they draw from the righteous principles they are committed to. Self-disciplined people do not like anyone from the outside having to check them. Not because of ego, not because of pride, not because of arrogance, but because they want to be in order from the inside out, to prove that they have graduated out of discipleship into apostleship.

Self-discipline is doing what we should do when we should do it, whether we feel like doing it or not. Self-discipline is doing whatever we have to do as long as we need to do it, until we get to where we want to be. Self-disciplined people do not quit when they are tired. They quit when they are done. Self-disciplined people organize all their knowledge, energy, strength and resources and fight with it until the goal is met. Self-discipline allows one to maintain action. The Self-disciplined one's mindset is that 'I'm in the world but not of the world.' Self-disciplined people do what is right. Self-discipline is the ability to work toward a goal systematically and progressively until its attainment. Popularity does not override principle. Brown nosing is not the way of a self-disciplined person. People pleasing is not the way of a self-disciplined person.

To move forward with an intentional life, we must graduate past being a people pleaser, to being one that does what they do to please God and God alone. Self-disciplined people put morality over conformity. Morality is doing what is right regardless of what everybody else is doing. Conformity is doing what everybody else is doing regardless to what is right. Romans 12:2 *"Be ye not conformed to this world: but be ye transformed by the renewing of your mind, that ye may prove what is that good, and acceptable, and perfect. will of God."* Self-disciplined people are not *creatures* of circumstances. They are *creators* of circumstances. Self-disciplined people are not affected by what others are doing. ***Self-disciplined people are all cause and never effect.***

Self-disciplined people are not chess pieces. Self-disciplined people are chess players. They are chess masters; they move the pieces. Self-disciplined people do not need to feel good to do good. They do good so they will feel good. Self-disciplined people do not wait for the spirit to move them. They move the spirit! Self-disciplined people, even though they are not the master, they handle themselves like they are the master. Self-disciplined people are lenient and merciful on others, but hard on themselves.

Epilogue

The Most Honorable Elijah Muhammad teaches that Allah (God) is the Creator of everything in the universe, including Himself; that Allah (God), is Self-created. The Most Honorable Elijah Muhammad teaches that there was a time period, in the history of the universe, before time began, there were three things in the universe, the *thought of God, electricity and material darkness.* The most mysterious force known to man, to this day, is electricity. The Holy Qur'an uses some metaphors or this material darkness. One of them is black mud. Another one is sounding Clay.

It is called *material* darkness, so it was a substantive darkness. The other thing present was electricity. Then there was the thought of God. It was the thought of God that maneuvered, directed, the electricity causing it to strike one of the dead atoms in the material darkness at the right place and at the right time. When the electricity struck that one atom, the electrical charge from the strike became the power of the atom. Today they say the power of an atom is found in its electrons. When you look at the word electron and electricity, you can tell that they are related to another. Electricity was the parent electron became the offspring. The atom that was once nothing or without aim and purpose began revolving (rotating) in space—in the darkness.

By the Law of Centripetal Force, the atom began spinning and drawing other atoms unto itself. The atom that was struck, then began loaning to the other atoms some of its power. The orbiting electrons in the nucleus of the atom began giving power to all the other atoms. Those atoms then began developing and joining on with the other atoms, giving life to one another creating molecules. Molecules began spinning and became cells. The cells continued to revolve, spinning until they produced an organ called the brain. Then the organ called the brain began bringing all the other organs into existence. And from those organs, the first organism called a body was produced. Allah (God), Himself, was formed as the first human being to exist.

The Honorable Elijah Muhammad was taught by Master Fard Muhammad, that Allah created His home planet simultaneous to His own Self-Creation. Common sense says if there is nothing in existence but thought, electricity and this material darkness, and God is creating Himself and His home planet at the same time, whatever He is using to make Himself up out of, He is also making His home planet out of. Why do we think, when we attend a funeral, the reverend says from the Earth we came and to the Earth we shall return and then say ashes to ashes, dust to dust. Why? Because the same material that the human body is made of, the Earth is made of.

If we take a globe and lay it flat and place a human being next to it, we can observe that the same way the veins and arteries move through the human body, lakes, rivers, and streams move through the Earth. The planet has fresh water called lakes and rivers, and salt water called seas and oceans. We have in the human body fresh water called saliva and blood. We also have salt water, called sweat and tears. The salt water and the fresh water in the Earth is in us.

The molecular structure of the bone of the human being is just like the rock of the Earth. The molecular structure of the water of the Earth is just like the blood of the human being. If we look at the vegetation of the Earth and compare it molecularly, it has the exact same structure as the flesh of the human being. This is why when we take a leaf from a tree and place it next to our hand, we will notice that the leaf has lines like our hand does. Why, because the leaf is at the end of the branch connected to the fruit that is produced from the tree. It is the hand of the human being that produces the fruits of our labor. We are all the same, from the same Earth.

The Holy Qur'an says that Allah (God) created the male and the female; two twin halves of a single essence. The single essence, the original material is the mind of God, Himself. So, if the only thing that existed was Allah (God) and the planet and everything we see is a product of the planet, the Honorable Minister Louis Farrakhan explains it like this, *"We are living in the very mind of God right now and don't even know it."* *"For in him we live and move and have our being..."* Acts 17:28

As we developed and grow by proper use of the mathematics of the mind, we too can possess that thought of God like the originator. The originator used the tool of electricity, guided by his mind to make war with this darkness, and bring into existence, Himself and the universe. Likewise, we must use the thought of God that we possess and the tool of our spirit, passion, drive, electricity to make war with darkness. The originator was able to create himself as God. What will happen if we use our thought of God, and electricity to wage war on darkness? Like the Originator, we can come out of this war, a god!

In a message titled, *__What is Your Role?__* The Honorable Minister Louis Farrakhan lays out the chief characteristics that made The Originator so successful.

The Characteristics of The Originator

1. He had Vision

2. He was Patient (it took Him eons and eons of time to create Himself)

3. He was a Warrior (went to war with the darkness)

4. Wise

5. Organized

6. Hard-working

7. A Producer

Words from The Honorable Minister Louis Farrakhan
(Explaining the power of Thought, Ideas, Creativity and Vision)

An idea is a well-developed thought. Ideas are different from thoughts. Ideas, like thoughts, exist in the mind, potentially or actually, as a product of mental activity. You cannot have an idea or thought, and your mind is not active. Brain waves on a machine that scans the activity of your mind, of your brain, shows an electrical energy in the brain that says [indicates] 'this [the brain or mind] is alive. 'Electrical energy in the brain allows the brain to do what the brain is designed to do—*Create thought*. Create images. Create pictures.

Once you have a thought, that is a concept. When you say sister has conceived. What do you mean? She's pregnant. Conception is not the baby. {the} Conception has all the necessary ingredients to make the baby but now it needs a period of gestation and growth, in the darkness of the womb, so that conception becomes a fully developed child, baby, fetus. When thought germinates in the mind, if you do not continue to think on the thought; then the thought, without more thought, only is a thought that comes and goes. And you will say, when somebody else comes up with the [same] thought, but thinks on the thought, they "stole my idea." Wait a minute fool, you don't have a corner on thought, on image. Many of you have good thoughts but you do nothing about [them]. So, the thought [then] was an opportunity that you blew because you didn't do by the thought what you [should] have done. You got to think on the thought and thinking on the thought is feeding the thought.

Then, the thought develops into an idea and that idea has with it a plan, a scheme, a method of fulfilling and concretizing what was a mental image, that had the potential; but now you want to actualize what you have envisioned. But if you develop the thought into an idea, and still will not work the idea, then God will give the idea to somebody else who will fulfill the idea and fulfill the vision brought by the idea.

After the thought brings up a concept, you have *conceived*. Most people talk 'the thought 'and the thought gets lost. Like showing a baby before the baby is a baby. Who wants to see a clot, but an abortionist? Most times when we get a thought, we speak it before we think on the thought. Get it [the thought] developed and it must develop in darkness, like the womb of the female, the womb of the mind--develop your idea, then develop the method, the plan of execution.

The idea will bring up a picture of the completed thing; the picture is in your brain. You can draw it on a piece of paper. So that you can keep the vision before your eyes but putting it on paper isn't actualizing the vision. The vision is only actualized when you bring it into concrete reality. How do you bring it into concrete reality? First, without faith you can't work the vision. Even if you see it, you gotta now believe that you can bring it. Believe! Not only believe in God but believe in yourself. Believe that you can do or accomplish what you envision that must be done; but belief alone is not of any value unless belief is translated into practice or work and it is belief joined by work that concretizes the vision.

Once you hear the word and meet the man. The man and the word are one. But the man, understand the man is the key to unlock the word. You can't take in the word and leave the man. You gotta take the man who brings the word and then study the man for the man is the word in action. And therefore, when you study the man and feed on the word then the love that you have in your heart for the man is the key to unlock the power of the word.

The word is light. Belief is compared to light. Now the word of God is light. The Holy Qur'an says "Allah is the light of those who believe He brings them out of darkness into light..." So, the belief is compared to light. Now the word of god is light. When you believe in the word that is light upon light. The word is light. Faith in the word is also light. If you hear the word, you are also receiving light but if you don't believe then you can't open the power of the word that you are receiving. It can't benefit you because you don't believe. If you believe, then there is a tendency to carry into practice your faith. So, faith is light upon light. Which magnifies the power in the word and gives the believer the power of his faith and the power of the word. And the power times the power is the ability to do the work that God has put upon us to bring into reality the, vision

Bible References

James 2:14" Prayer without works is dead."

Romans 8:28 "All things work together for the good for them that do love the Lord."

Matthew 9:4" And Jesus knowing their thoughts said, Wherefore think ye evil in your hearts?"

Matthew 18:20, "Wherever there are two or more gathered together in my name, there I am also."

1John 2:19 "They went out from us, but they were not of us; for if they had been of us, they would no doubt have continued with us: but they went out, that they might be made manifest..."

John 10:10 "I came that you may have life and have it more, abundantly"

3 John 1:2 "Above all things, I wish that you would prosper. And be in good health, even as thy soul prospereth"

John 1:1 'In the beginning was the word. The word was God, the word was with God, the world became flesh.'

Philippians 2:5 "Let this mind be in you, the same mind that was in Christ Jesus."

Proverbs 23:7 "As a man thinketh in his heart, so is he."

Luke 17:21 "The Kingdom of God (Heaven) is within you."

Mark 10:8 "Thou good master." "Why calleth thou me good? There's none good but the Father."

John 5:30 "I of my own self can do nothing."

John 16:13 "Whatsoever I heareth, that shall I speak."

John 14:31 "Whatsoever the Father commandeth me to do, that shall I do."

John 6:38 " It's not my will that I do, but it is the will of the Father who hath sent me."

Romans 12:2 " Be ye not conformed to this world: but be ye transformed by the renewing of your mind, that ye may prove what is that good, and acceptable, and perfect. Will of God."

Job 1:7 "...The Lord said unto Satan, Whence comest thou? Then Satan answered the LORD, and said, From going to and fro in the earth, and from walking up and down in it."

Holy Qur'an Refrences

3:54 " And (the Jews) planned and Allah (also) planned. And Allah is the best of planners."

103 " By the time, surely man is in loss Except those who believe and do good and exhort one another to truth, and exhort one another to patience."

71:13 " What is the matter with you that you hope not for greatness from your Lord?"

20:2 Allah (God) says, "We did not reveal the Qur'an to you that you would be unsuccessful."

23:1 "You can tell the believers, they are the successful ones."

9:72 " And the greatest of all is Allah's goodly pleasure. That is the grand achievement."

13:11 " Surely Allah changes not the condition of a people, until they change their own condition."

11:7 "And He it is who created the heavens and the earth in six periods. And his thrown of power..."

13:11 " Allah changes not the condition of a people until that people change their own condition."

53:39 "Man shall have nothing, but that which he strives for."

84:6 "And soon you shall see the ends for which men strive."

About The Author

Born on November 21, 1974, Brother Nuri Muhammad joined the Nation of Islam in 1992 at seventeen years of age. Having a strong will and mind and a desire to do something positive for himself, his family and his people, Brother Nuri was consistently active in all aspects of the Mosque and became a fervent student of the Teachings of the Most Honorable Elijah Muhammad.

In August of 2005, the Honorable Minister Louis Farrakhan referred to Brother Nuri as anointed and gave him the Holy Name "Nuri," which comes from Al-Nur, meaning "the light."

Brother Nuri cherishes July 5 as the anniversary of his marriage to his wife Sis. Terri Muhammad, who is his greatest support in The Mission. They are the proud parents of three children.

For more on Nuri Muhammad visit his website:
Nurimuhammad.com
Instagram & Facebook @Nurimuhammad
Twitter @BrotherNuri